They Called Me
Boston

PATRICK SHANAHAN

ISBN 978-1-0980-8804-0 (paperback)
ISBN 978-1-0980-8922-1 (digital)

Christian Faith Publishing, Inc.
832 Park Avenue
Meadville, PA 16335
www.christianfaithpublishing.com

Printed in the United States of America

My Brother's Smile

By the light of my brother's smile,
a million stories begin to unfold.
Some of them I could tell you,
but most of them are his own.
Stories of love, pain, strength and courage;
Stories of his inner soul---
A soul so bright and full of life,
that these stories should be told.

Through him I have been taught,
and I have learned, that this life
is not only your own.
The world is full of taking and using,
but it is the giving you should behold.
The giving of love and kindness,
and always a hand up or a friendly word.

I have grown with this man,
I call my brother.
And my life is enriched because of his love.
I cherish his life of stories,
and I look forward to the ones not told.

By the light of my brother's smile,
I have learned to love the unknown.
Because I know if these stories are lived
through him, all that will be told,
are stories of honesty, love and laughter---
Stories of a man's soul.

January 5, 1999
Love, Buzzer

HELP ME! PLEASE help me! Lying on my back, I tried to roll over, but I couldn't move. I was staring out of a blurry window, wondering where I was. I yelled for someone to lower my legs, hoping that would allow me to roll on my side. A tired lady, dressed as a nurse, entered my room. She assured me that my legs were fine. Then she suggested, "If you want to rest, press the red button on the right side of your bed." As she exited, I pressed the red button, and euphoria kicked in. The response from the red button became my favorite; it freed me from the reality that I was in a hospital somewhere. As I fell back into a calm coma, my legs felt like they were up in the air again. This time, I pressed a button labeled "Help," and a different nurse entered with a friendly smile.

"My name is Mary, and I will be your night nurse," she said with a sweet voice. I tried to lift my covers, but my arms were too heavy. I asked Mary if she could help me. She laughed and suggested that I stopped pressing the morphine button. Mary showed me my legs at the end of the bed. I asked her why they felt like they were up in the air, but her explanation made no sense at the time. She called me Boston and sat down next to me.

Chapter 1

Born and Raised

ON SEPTEMBER 14, 1967, a young Irish couple named me Patrick Daniel Shanahan, at least that's what my birth certificate says. My real name is PJ.

The story that my mother recalls is this: "Hang in there, just keep breathing!" Wootie said. Her aunt Wootie drove her to the front door of Providence Hospital, Holyoke, Massachusetts, in an old Pontiac. As the doors flew open, so did my mother's womb, just in time for the doctor to unravel my umbilical cord that was wrapped around my neck.

"Just keep breathing!" my mother prayed.

I was born and raised in a small Irish Catholic town; Holyoke, Massachusetts is in my blood. I was the third son, the prodigal son, the son they wished was a daughter. I was conceived at a party on New Year's Eve. Thank God my little sister was born two years later. I thought my parents were going to start dressing me up in skirts.

Chapter 2

Historic Holyoke

WE WERE A tight-knit, fun-loving Irish family that did everything together. Jerome Frances "Jerry" was born on March 22, 1964; Christopher William "Chris" was born on April 20, 1965; and Laura Ann "Buzzer" was born on November 28, 1969. We grew up in the highlands of Holyoke in a two-family house on 68 Fairfield Ave. The upstairs apartment was converted into an indoor playground. The hockey room had boarded up windows and linoleum floors so the puck would slide easier. There was a ping pong table in another room, one big bedroom with velvet glow-in-the-dark wallpaper, and a full kitchen, large enough to make plenty of popcorn.

The main house had two floors with wide winding stairs that led to a large open area on the first floor, perfect for skidding out. We drove our mini Budweiser cars down the stairs often. My favorite part of 68 Fairfield Ave was the large backyard with an above ground pool; the laughter from all of the neighborhood kids, splashing around on hot summer days in the early '70s, still echoes in the highlands of Holyoke. Fairfield Ave is listed in the historic section of Holyoke. It should be listed in the hysterical section.

Many mischievous boys grew up on Fairfield Ave, but my favorite were the six Kane brothers. We played hockey in the streets and football on the narrow islands with the pavement in bounds for painful touchdowns. We shared one pair of skis with boots attached to the bindings and carved a narrow, steep path in the woods behind the Marian center where the nuns lived. At the bottom of the trail, we built a large jump; there was no way of avoiding it. I loved the adrenaline as I flew through the air, but I usually came out of the large boots and tumbled down the rest of the hill. I truly believe the nuns were reciting their rosaries just for us. My favorite was gliding behind moving cars as we held onto their bumpers on snow-covered roads, otherwise known as bumper riding.

My bumper riding career ended abruptly after the Christmas of 1975. My mother bought me new gloves for a present that year with Santa's name on them. I was holding on tightly to the bumper of a Chevy on a freezing cold day in early January, and when I let go, my gloves froze to the bumper. I watched the Chevy drive away with my new gloves attached to it. When I finally arrived home, my fingers were purple, and my mother was extremely inquisitive. I told her that I lost them somewhere. I learned at an early age that I will never get away with lying.

She packed us kids up to go grocery shopping. As we parked our car and began to exit, the Chevy, with my frozen gloves still attached to its bumper, pulled in next to us.

"Hey, those gloves look familiar!" my mother yelled. She was into natural consequences that winter; therefore, my fingers remained cold and purple for a few weeks until her conscience got the best of her. That was my first experience learning about God's great sense of humor.

My second valuable lesson from God came from trying to make up for disrespecting my mother during the winter. On Mother's Day, my little sister and I decided to steal a flower arrangement from outside of Magri's neighborhood store and gave it to my mother as a gift. Little did we know, it was a cemetery log. That didn't go over so well, especially when she knew that we didn't have any money. "Thou shall not steal" became my first real sin as a young Irish lad.

Chapter 3

My Only Grandparent

MY GRANDMOTHER "LIBBY" used to say, "PJ, you are the best kid at a party, but there isn't a party today." I always thought she was giving me a compliment.

Grandmother Elizabeth "Libby" Shanahan raised her four sons on Nonotuck street. Her house was close to our neighborhood. My Grandfather Jerome died before I was born. My dad was only eighteen years old when his father died; therefore, I learned about my grandfather by listening to epic stories as we looked at pictures of his life's accomplishments. He was an amazing baseball player growing up, and he pursued his passion in college. He played third base for Holy Cross College in Worcester, Massachusetts, and was drafted by the St. Louis Browns in 1931.

His greatest accomplishment was marrying Elizabeth Mannix. My grandmother lived in Worcester, Massachusetts, and her father owned a restaurant. My great-grandfather Cornelius Mannix named his restaurant Mannix and Jones. The Holy Cross baseball team used to eat there in the 1930s. Before Jerome graduated in 1931, he met my beautiful grandmother Libby while she was working there. They fell in love, a love that blessed them with four loving boys. Neal was the oldest; then my father, Jerome "Jogger," a couple years younger; William "Billy"; and the youngest, Daniel "Danny."

When I was growing up, Neal moved to Alaska as a volunteer for the domestic Peace Corp that was launched by President John F. Kennedy. He taught and learned in coastal Eskimo villages along the Yukon River. It was in Gambell, Alaska, on the St. Lawrence island, west of mainland Alaska in the Bering Sea, that native villag-ers trusted my uncle Neal to hunt whales with them; they hunted back then in the traditional way, by hand, in handmade boats with seal skin stretched over whalebone. My favorite gift from Alaska was our whale-skin toboggan. It was the fastest sled in the highlands. Neal also developed a curriculum in schools that helped identify and teach children affected by alcoholism. He met his wife, Kathy, in Alaska and was blessed with two sons, Lee and Jeremy.

Danny truly fascinated me with his singing, poetry, and med-itation. He would come and go, leaving me with stories to ponder on from his trips to Alaska and living in an ashram in India. He eventually settled down when he married his soulmate, Carla, who is a professional singer. Their combined voices bless all who can hear.

Uncle Billy lives in Holyoke and is always a blessing to be around. Uncle Billy married Mary, blessed with three kids, Kara, Owen, and Andy. We are all blessed to be Shanahans.

Chapter 4

Early Days and Mischievous Ways

THE ELEMENTARY SCHOOL we attended was called Highland School. We walked or rode our bikes to school, depending on the weather. It was the only school that all four of us attended at the same time. We moved from Fairfield Ave to Bemis Heights after my fifth grade year.

There were many changes to adjust to at that stage in my life, but the blessing was going to a new school called E. N. White. I walked to school with my new neighbors and met some of my best friends for life; Macker, the Lavelle brothers, and Beaker all lived in the nearby neighborhoods. We developed lifelong relationships, and I'm truly grateful for them.

The most significant adjustment was when my mother started working. My mother's father, Larry, owned a liquor store, and she inherited the business after he died young. During the Fairfield Ave days of growing up, my father ran the store while my mother stayed home with us. After our move, she decided to take over the store, and my father became a wine salesman. They were constantly working. Thank God for Sundays.

The one constant in the Shanahan family was Sunday Mass at Holy Cross Church. I truly looked forward to attending church as a family. We all sat together in a long wooden pew. Many other families from the Highlands attended the same Mass, including our good friends, the Pappy brothers. I loved seeing all of our Christian friends. It was Holyoke Highlands in its finest hour.

Holy Cross was my sanctuary. I was baptized there, made my first communion, and was confirmed to Catholicism within the beautiful old stone church. It was safe to confess my childhood sins at Holy Cross; there were plenty of opportunities to sin growing up in the Highlands of Holyoke, at least for this mischievous Irish lad. My favorite part of Catholicism is forgiveness. "Go and sin no more," Jesus said. I tried to obey his demand, but unfortunately, I took it as a suggestion some days.

My mischievous behaviors took on greater risks in my teenage years. Sports became secondary as I began partying in the woods of Holyoke. On the weekends, there was always a keg party to attend in the nearby reservoir at the bottom of Mt. Tom. At the age of fourteen, a few friends and I built a fort near the Upper Tee slope on the Mt. Tom ski area. Our fort was large enough for six people; it had a fireplace made out of stones and a little chimney from an old pipe we dragged up on the mountain. The fort looked like a bunch of broken pine branches that had fallen on top of each other. We marked a tree near the top of the trail so we could ski to our fort. When our local ski mountain opened during the winter months, we had our own sanctuary to hide out and party.

The Mt. Tom ski area was dear to my heart. The owner, Jimmy Joe O'Connell, introduced my father to my mother when they were teenagers. The ski mountain was a favorite for many families but especially for us, Shanahans. It was open day and night; therefore, our parents used to drop us off early morning on the weekends and pick us up later at night. That was until we started driving. Then the shenanigans really began.

The mountain closed at 10:00 p.m., and lights were shut off by 10:30 p.m. My favorite times were hiding in our fort until the lights were off, then we would ski down the mountain in complete darkness. A few epic full moons are still radiant in my heart's memory.

With older brothers driving, it allowed this little brother more time to adventure around the city. They would drive me around with their friends and bring me to parties on the other side of Holyoke. Then it was validated that all of Holyoke liked to party. But the greatest party of all was our famous St. Patrick's weekend.

The Saturday after March 17 was Holyoke's St. Patrick's road race, a ten-kilometer that worked its way from downtown up and around Holyoke Community College, past the Holyoke Soldiers Home, and the finish line was in front of St. Patrick's Chapel. Many champion runners, avid runners, and amateur joggers ran the course as the majority of Holyoke partied on the sidelines cheering them on. One and done, I ran it one year and wore high-top green chucks, thinking I was cool; I lost three toenails that race. On Sunday, Holyoke's doors were opened as all families convened for our famous St. Patrick's parade. It didn't matter what side of town you were from; we were all Holyokers celebrating the patron saint of Ireland.

Chapter 5

The Trigger

THERE WERE TWO junior high schools when I grew up in Holyoke, Massachusetts. The kids from the highlands and the north side of downtown went to Lynch; that's where I met the Sweeney brothers, best friends for life. The south side of Holyoke went to Peck. We competed against each other during sporting events. It was a blessing to make friends on and off the fields of competition. Youth sports were a great way to make strong bonds with the kids from downtown for me. My favorite sports were soccer, hockey, tennis, and baseball.

Holyoke's nickname is "The Paper City." In the late nineteenth century and early twentieth century, Holyoke was the largest producer of stationery, writing, and archival goods in the world! The western bank of the Connecticut River flowed along the railroad tracks that stretched from New York to Vermont. Holyoke built a damn that produced hydroelectric power in tandem with the Holyoke Canal System. Along the canals, there were many apartment blocks built that provided inexpensive apartments initially for the paper mill workers.

Many Irish families migrated to Holyoke to work in the paper mills. Holyoke was predominantly Irish up until my junior high school days. As the industry changed, so did downtown Holyoke. The majority of the apartment blocks became occupied by many different cultures, speaking different languages and fighting over the limited jobs as the mills closed down.

The economy took a big hit; therefore, more violent crimes began to happen. It was a risk to walk around certain parts of downtown Holyoke. I learned the hard way through one of my good friends—God bless, KD.

My friend lived downtown with his single mother. We became close friends as we attended Lynch Junior High School together. He was a good-looking, fun-loving kid that started dating one of my girlfriends from my new neighborhood. The last night I saw him, we were in eighth grade, and all of us were loving life on a Saturday night. As he was leaving, we hugged it out, and I remember saying, "Look forward to seeing you Monday morning at school."

As my friends and I walked into Lynch on Monday morning, the principal pulled us into his office. With a concerned look on his face, he asked us if we heard what happened on Sunday night. None of us had any idea what he was about to share. The principal had the local *Holyoke Transcript Telegram* newspaper in his hands. With a tear in his eyes, he told us that our friend Kevin was shot in the back and died early Monday morning!

Adult condolences fell short of comfort that morning. Numbness took over, as oxygen was depleted from the hallways of John J. Lynch Junior High School. Death introduced herself for the first time in my brief fourteen years of life. It was the beginning of my true dialogue with God. All of my prayers have been rehearsed, practiced, and recited up to that point; the words of grief, anger, confusion, and trust were flowing from my broken heart. "Lord Jesus, I trust that you know what you are doing and have heavenly reasons for my friend. Amen."

Chapter 6

High School Shenanigans

I ENTERED HOLYOKE High School with good intentions. That lasted five minutes. After the principal cornered me, he stuck his finger in my chest, and he warned me that he would not put up with any of my shenanigans. I guess my older brothers caused him some gray hairs during their days under his ruling.

We were all athletes, decent students, but we were Shanahan's capable of shenanigans! My oldest brother Jerry was All-Western Mass. Hockey, second in his class academically, but showed up intoxicated at the senior dance; therefore, he was suspended and couldn't attend his senior prom. I entered high school on the heels of his graduation. I guess the principal wasn't practicing Catholicism. I asked him after he cornered me if he believed in forgiveness. That earned me my first of many detentions.

The real trouble wasn't happening in the halls of Holyoke High School; it was primarily in our Shanahan home. I sensed some trouble between my loving parents. The arguments were getting louder, my father's traveling as a wine salesman became extensive, and my mother became more distracted running the liquor store. All of our needs were cared for. It was the spiritual that was lacking. It was difficult for all of us to attend church together. We, as a family, were in trouble.

It was 1982, shortly after my sixteenth birthday, that my parents decided to separate. It felt like a bomb went off in our living room, and we all ran in different directions. Jerry ran to Union College, my father ran to Grandma Libby's house, my little sister ran upstairs to my room, and my older brother Chris climbed out the window to go party with his friends; my mother drove to the liquor store and stayed busy.

Divorce was foreign back in the 80s. None of my friend's parents were divorced, so they had no clue what to say. They just passed me a joint, handed me a beer, and turned up the music. And I loved them for that.

Music became my therapy. I was introduced to the Grateful Dead by my older brothers. In the song "Franklin's Tower," my favorite verse is "When you get confused, listen to the music play." A girl friend of mine, talented in her ways, embroidered the *Steal Your Face* Grateful Dead symbol on the back of my jean jacket.

I went to my first live Dead show at the age of sixteen with my best friends, the Sweeney brothers and the Lavelle brothers. The concert was at the New Haven Coliseum, and they opened the show with Alabama Getaway. It was an intense spiritual experience, a strange trip they say. The Grateful Dead seasonal tours became a divine "getaway" for me and my siblings. Since the church was no longer a welcoming experience for our divorced family in the 1980s, the Dead scene became my church.

My academics became secondary in tenth grade; my pot smoking was primary. It became my medicine; it calmed my ADHD. I was smoking before school, during school, and definitely after school. I was caught smoking before the Thanksgiving day rally and was suspended for two weeks. For some reason, my principal trusted me to tell my parents. Why ruin a good turkey? I didn't tell my mother until she came upstairs to wake me up in the morning that I was supposed to return to school. That was my first day of working at our family liquor store. What else was she going to do with me for two weeks?

Legally, I couldn't work in the alcohol section of the store, thank God Massachusetts passed the bottle bill; therefore, I ran the redemption center. The Springfield Liquor Mart became my daily hangout. I met all kinds of characters; my favorites were the old-timers who knew my grandparents. Within weeks of working, I heard more stories about my mother's side of the family from customers than I did from my humble, quiet mom.

My grandfather, Larry Gobeille, married my grandmother, Alice Dillon, in 1942 before he left for World War II. He was a decorated Army war hero when he was discharged from fighting in France. Thank God he survived because his only daughter, my blessed mother, Carol, was born on December 19, 1943.

Larry had three siblings, two brothers named Gerry and Paul and his sister, Madeline. Gerry was the oldest Gobeille and also served in the military. Gerry was blessed with five kids, Liz, Richie, Jimmy, Eddie, and God bless Bob, who passed away young from a tragic accident. Dr. Paul married Jackie Lapanne, and we grew up with their beautiful family, Paul Jr., Tom, Steve, and their sister, Christine. Madeline married a local Irishman, Frank McKenna, and we were also blessed to grow up with their kids, Marry Ann, Carol, and John.

My Grandmother Alice Dillion had one brother named Buddy and two sisters, Mayme and Eileen "Wootie." Buddy married Helen, and they also opened a liquor store called Dillons; they had four sons, Jim, John, Billy, Bob, and a daughter, Diane. Jim was born with a compromised heart condition and died in his teenage years. Billy died from a car accident in his twenties, but the youngest Dillon, Bob, became my best friend. Bob married Christine and are blessed with two sons, Josh and Billy.

My mother's aunt Wootie married Dave Manning and was blessed with a son named DJ and a daughter, Eileen. Eileen married an Irish character named Maurice Cavanaugh; they were blessed with three beautiful kids, Brian, Danny, and Meghan that were younger than us, but I always loved seeing them. DJ married Mary Lou, and they adopted a daughter, Sarah, and a son, Taylor.

The Springfield Liquor Mart dates back to 1949, when my mother's parents, Larry and Alice, opened the doors, a short sixteen years after prohibition. My grandfather Larry ran the store until he died young in 1959, then my grandmother Alice took it over until she died in 1965. My mother was the only child and too young to operate the liquor store; my great aunt Mayme Ryback took care of the business until my mother and father took over. Mayme's husband, Loui, owned a famous grocery store in downtown Holyoke called Rybacks. Loui was like a grandfather to us, Shanahan kids.

There I was sixteen years old, suspended from tenth grade for smoking pot and working at our family liquor store. I did not see my circumstances as a problem; I thought of it as a blessing. The redemption center was built on to the side of the liquor store, and it was mine to manage. I became responsible for my time while earning my own money. The greatest blessing was gratitude.

I was always a thankful kid for what my parents provided, but I became more grateful as I witnessed the family business in full operation. Managing trustworthy employees and keeping customers happy on a daily basis wasn't always easy. My mother taught me invaluable lessons within a liquor store.

Customers first, employees have to earn trust, and have fun while working! These were my mother's phrases that she constantly reminded me of. My mother taught me more than she will ever know. As she struggled emotionally during the early stages of divorce, her family was always a priority. Unconditional love came naturally for her.

To complicate my sophomore year, I was confirmed to Catholicism in the spring. I made my confirmation at Holy Cross Church, but for some Catholic reason, I felt like I was committing a sin. The same time I was confirming my faith, "the hierarchy of the Church" was asking my mother to annul her marriage. I was confused, and instead of confronting God with my confusion over religion, I ignored the church.

I continued to challenge my mother's love as I stumbled through my high school years. My parents decided to send me to a boarding school for my junior year. Within the first few months at Wilbraham Monson Academy, I was put on probation for a coed violation. I got caught in my girlfriend's room after hours and was placed on weekend restriction. I had to report to a teacher every hour, beginning at 8:00 a.m. on Saturday until 10:00 p.m. After the first weekend, I asked a friend from Holyoke to come visit me at 7:05 p.m. He picked me up in his car with a cooler of beers, and by 7:15, we were pulled over by the Wilbraham police. It didn't look good when the nice policeman escorted me in for my check-in.

I was told to pack my bags and prepare for expulsion. As my new friends Fritz and Art helped me, a school counselor entered my room. She introduced herself, then proceeded to tell me that my mother loves me and was concerned for my well-being. The tears flowed for the next hour until my mother arrived. We drove silently back to Holyoke, but the silence was therapeutic for the both of us.

My little sister greeted me with laughter, and the Holyoke High principal wished me good luck. I was back home. I made amends by attending every class and exhibiting gratitude. I finished my junior year on a positive note. I was determined to graduate with my 1985 classmates. I had to take extra classes my senior year and was ineligible to play varsity hockey; therefore, I joined the ski team.

Winter of 1985 proved to be a divine season. I fell in love with racing gates; also, I fell in love with a Catholic girl. Holyoke High and Holyoke Catholic High School traveled on the same bus to Berkshire East ski mountain every Thursday for races. CC's beauty was captivating. There is nothing more attractive than a beautiful girl that can ski well. We initially met on the back of the bus, then rode the chair lifts together. Chair lifts are made for intimacy. Thank God I couldn't play hockey.

We enjoyed each other's company throughout the ski season, attended many parties together in the spring, and I went to her senior prom. As graduation became near, we decided to spend some time with our own classmates. I'll never forget my Holyoke High senior keg party in the south side of Holyoke's reservoir.

I attended the party with the senior guys that I used to play soccer with, including AW. We played on little league teams together. He was a good friend to many. As a group of us stumbled out of the woods together, we acknowledged that it was our last Saturday night before graduation; we hugged it out, said our goodbyes, and I remember saying, "See you Monday for our senior pictures."

We were all planning to walk home in our different directions. AW and BF were neighbors, so they were walking together. As they were on the road, a guy they knew, driving a fast car, asked them if they wanted a ride. The driver was showing off how fast his car drove and flipped it, trying to make a sharp turn. AW died during the accident. I heard about the tragedy the next morning. Once again, Death introduced herself, captured my mind, and tormented my heart at a young age. God bless AW and his family.

The funeral was packed with my classmates and half of Holyoke. As I entered the Blessed Sacrament Church on the south side of Holyoke, instinctually, I blessed myself with the holy water. I can't honestly say it reminded me of being baptized, but I can say it awakened my Catholicism. In that vulnerable moment, I heard God say, "It's okay, I love you!" That's all that I continued to hear. I couldn't hear the priest's words; they were muffled by the intense sobbing around me; therefore, I continued my grieving dialogue with God. "Dear Jesus, I trust you know what you are doing. Please congratulate my friend and tell him I miss him already."

There were many mixed emotions at our graduation. I never thought it was possible to feel joy and sorrow at the same time. My heart was conflicted, and my mind was set on loving every minute of my life, but I was a reckless mess heading off to college, somewhere.

Chapter 7

College Take One

OBVIOUSLY, I WAS not recruited for college. I had two choices, University of Tampa or Niagara University; palm trees, pretty girls, and beaches or power lines, freezing weather, and a dangerous waterfall? I arrived in Florida, ready to party. Two ROTC roommates greeted me with suspicion of my long hair and tie-dye T-shirt. It was not a welcoming beginning of college. The facial expressions on their parents' faces were priceless. I guess they never saw a "Dead Head" before?

The very first weekend was the violent force that set my reckless attitude in turbulent motion. After partying on Friday night at the local establishment and meeting new friends, I retreated back to my dorm room to crash. At 2:30 a.m., our RA keyed into our room and demanded that we grab the essentials and prepare to evacuate.

"Hurricane Gloria is on her way!" He loudly warned.

"I'm from Holyoke, Massachusetts, what the hell are essentials for a hurricane?" I remember yelling. My roommates were in fatigues and already headed out the door. I had an old ripped pair of jeans, a long-sleeve tie-dye shirt, and a bandana on; I grabbed my underarm deodorant and wrapped my tapestry around me like a cape. As I was walking out of my room, I saw my roommate's swimming goggles and thought that they could be "the essentials?"

When I walked outside the dorm, the rain was coming down sideways, wind was screaming, and so was everyone else. We were instructed to get in the campus vans that pulled up in front. As I waited with some hysterical girls, a pickup truck, with three cute girls in the front and two guys in the open back, drove by. I decided that the numbers looked good; therefore, with my goggles on, tapestry cape flowing in the wind, I ran and dove in the back of the truck. That was the beginning of a lifelong friendship with Maz. I introduced myself, and we drove away to my new friend's parents' condo in a fairly safe neighborhood away from the bay. It was a crazy, emotional two-day Hurricane Gloria party for me and Maz; the new girlfriends remained anxious.

I survived my first hurricane, experienced two unexpected deaths of young friends, and now had to retreat into the battle zone of my own dorm room. It didn't help my situation by taking my roommate's swimming goggles without permission. They were definitely tattered from Gloria's mighty winds, but I thought he wouldn't notice. I planned to place them back on his dresser when I returned, but as I entered the room, standing stern in his fatigues, he was waiting for me. His room was in impeccable order; therefore, he knew his goggles were missing. That was the true beginning of our roommate war.

He got the RA involved, and with both roommates dressed for battle, the demands echoed across campus. They rudely gave me two options: either I move out or they turn me into the campus police. With a crooked smile on my face, I pleaded my case that I needed the essentials in order to survive my first hurricane. I offered to buy him new ones, but the crime was already committed. My only defense was to seek forgiveness, but he wasn't practicing Catholicism either. I reminded them that I was from Holyoke and had nowhere else to move to.

I was put on dorm probation, and my roommates plotted their next move. I continued to live in a hostile situation, but they didn't have to turn me into the campus police.

The Grateful Dead announced their fall tour. It included two shows in Florida within driving distance and two shows in Richmond, Virginia, that friends from Holyoke were planning to attend. Being a good Deadhead, I plotted my "getaway." I needed to buy my tickets, pay for an overnight eight-hour train ride to Richmond, and have extra money to party. I had some book money reserved, but I needed some more spare change.

Late one night, I decided to borrow my friend's snorkel gear with his permission and dove into the campus fountain filled with spare change. With flippers on, mask, and snorkel, wet shorts falling off because my pockets were filled with my train fare, I started to sneak back to my dorm room. All of a sudden, the campus police officer on patrol spotted me and put his golf cart sirens on. The chase was on!

I woke up in the campus jail with at least eighty dollars' worth of quarters on the table in front of me. The large campus officer was still laughing when I came to.

He said, "Your crazy white ass knocked yourself out and made it easy for me."

"I guess it's dangerous to try and run with flippers on, huh?" I responded.

"You have some explaining to do, son," he said. Because I entertained him, he went easy on me. I received campus probation and weekend campus cleanup duty.

The very next morning, after my roommates heard the embarrassing news, they shared their news. They were moving off-campus. God intervened on my behalf again. His divine mercy had my crazed attention. "Please forgive me, Lord, for I have sinned again. Sorry I borrowed my roommate's goggles without permission and stole from the campus fountain." I begged God with a smirk on my face. It was not my most sincere confession.

Still needing money for my fall tour, I held a dorm room tag sale and sold all of my neon beer signs hanging on my wall. The tour went as scheduled. With my Halloween mask on, I boarded my train at 8:00 p.m., destined for Richmond, Virginia. It was 1985, October 31. The first show, November 1, the Grateful Dead closed the second set with an epic version of "Gloria." It was another divine spiritual experience for me. My eight-hour train ride back to Tampa provided plenty of time to continue my dialogue with God. This time, it was genuinely grateful.

On my return back to U of Tampa, I received more blessings. My roommates moved out. I had a triple dorm room to myself. Our dorm was a converted nine-story hotel; Tampa Bay was within view from my window. My dorm room became a vacation destiny for many visitors from Holyoke; an extended spring break led to an extended summer break. I was not invited back to U of Tampa.

Chapter 8

The Balancing Act

I WAS ON my own now. If I wanted a college education, it was my financial responsibility. My high school romance reignited over the summer, and CC planned to attend UMass in the fall; therefore, I moved into an apartment in Amherst, Massachusetts, with a couple of friends that were UMass students, Noodles and Stanley. I enrolled in two classes at Holyoke Community College and started working at the liquor side of our family business.

I learned how to balance life's responsibilities. I actually enjoyed my college electives; it was my money, my future. I was the investment. All went well that first year on my own; many Dead Shows fulfilled my spiritual journey.

Chapter 9

New life

CC AND I shared much quality time together. During our Christmas break, we received an invite to ski in Utah. We had friends that lived in Midvale, Utah, and worked for the Snow Bird Resort. One of my friends dated my little sister. He easily sold the idea for us to move out there for a ski season. A six-month lease for a one-bedroom apartment on the bus route to Snow Bird was feasible; we flew out there with our skis, adventurous love in our hearts, and a game plan to work at the resort for our free ski pass.

We celebrated CC's twenty-first birthday in Utah, skied over ninety glorious days; fifty of them were in deep powder. I fell in love with the light deep snow. It was easy to love the Wasatch National Mountains. They reminded me of picture books with mountains sticking straight up off the page. The highest peak of the Wasatch National Mountains is Mt. Nebo; it is almost twelve thousand feet. Compared to Mt. Tom's 1,200 feet, to me, they appeared fictitious from a distance.

A highlight of my trip was when I climbed to the peak of Solitude Mountain with my friends and our ski gear. As I ascended to the peak at 10,400 feet above sea level, it took my breath away. Helicopters landed as I caught my breath; four skiers climbed out laughing at us. As they finished their hot coffees, we had the last laugh. We took full advantage of the fresh snow before they ruined it. It was an orgasmic ski day, making fresh tracks all the way to the slope side saloon.

The end of the season was near; therefore, CC and I discussed our transition back home. We acknowledged that we should continue pursuing our college degrees and to live with our separate friends.

After all, we were young and still had much to explore. I was going to miss the Wasatch National Mountains.

God made sure that they would always remain a special part of our lives. A week after we arrived back home, CC discovered some news that answered why she was sick in the mornings. I was on my way to Chicago with my best friends, Macker and Noodles, for the beginning of the 1988 Summer Grateful Dead tour. I received the phone call an hour before the first concert. "PJ, enjoy the shows, make it home safe please, you are going to be a father!" CC shared in a concerned tone.

Wow, what a ski trip, I thought. I shared the news with my friends and danced like it was my last Dead show. The reality of becoming a father really didn't sink in until I arrived back home and witnessed CC's heartbeat. It beat twice as loud!

I was only twenty years old and made many selfish decisions up to that stage in life. Still scarred from my parents' divorce, the eternal commitment of marriage scared me away from proposing to CC. The most righteous thing that I could do was get a full-time job with insurance. I knew, as the father, I would have to provide health insurance for our baby. At that time, the Springfield Liquor Mart couldn't offer insurance; therefore, my mother called in a favor with our local Budweiser distributor.

Within a week of the news, I was driving an Eagle Snack truck, delivering honey-roasted peanuts and Cape Cod potato chips. Williams Distributing owned the rights to sell snacks, as well as Budweiser products, throughout Western Massachusetts. It was the only full-time position available that would grant me insurance to cover the birth of our baby. My first account opened their doors at 4:00 a.m.; my first accident took a week. I backed into the Wonder Bread guy's truck at 3:45 a.m. I tried to bribe him with peanuts, but he wasn't having it. After a few more incidents involving the lack of good judgment, I was let go, but our insurance carried us through the year.

I experienced the most divine Christmas season that year. As an Irish Catholic, I celebrated the birth of Jesus every year. But in 1988, I was truly blessed to celebrate two amazing births. December 21st at 5:45 a.m., CC safely delivered a beautiful baby girl. The greatest gift was cutting the umbilical cord of Casey Elizabeth Shanahan; God was surely present. We decided to honor my grandmother with Casey's middle name, and her first name has a Grateful Dead influence. She was the most divine gift that Christmas.

Even though CC and I were planning to live separately, we decided to try to live as a family. I worked as many hours as I could at the liquor store and took one class at Holyoke Community College. My selfish side found time to party and go to many Dead shows. We took Casey to her first Dead show in a backpack at Giants Stadium on July 9, 1989. They opened the show with "Touch of Grey, I will get by, I will survive." Jerry sang brilliantly. It felt like he was singing to me; it was a strange trip.

On the way home, we had an argument over my selfishness because I wanted to continue partying after the concert. After the first year, we decided that it would be best that we lived separately. She suggested that I get out of town for a little while so she could adjust to a new schedule.

Chapter 10

Ski Therapy

THE ONLY OPTION that I could think of was to go on another ski trip; therefore, I called a Holyoke friend of mine, Toby, who was living in Steamboat Springs, Colorado. He invited me out to stay with him. I departed for Steamboat in November to get a job for the beginning of the ski season. I booked two returning flights; the first was on December 19, my beautiful mother's birthday. That allowed me to be home in time to prepare for Casey's birthday and truly celebrate Christmas with our families. The final trip home was on St. Patrick's Day; CC and I agreed that would be enough time away for her to create a healthy motherly routine.

The first stop when I arrived in Steamboat was the Gondola Liquor Store. After buying a bottle of Jack Daniels, I asked the clerk if they were looking for help. I told him that I ran a large liquor store at home. He called the owner, who lived in Texas, and put me on the phone with him. Within the first hour at Steamboat, I had a job as the night manager in a liquor store that was at the bottom of the mountain. *God was looking out for me*, I thought.

I skied everyday right into work, partied every night, but fell asleep thinking about Casey. The chairlift rides provided quality time to think about my life. But it also provided an opportunity to meet another girl. I was a conflicted young father.

Thank God for Casey's birthday party. CC and I spent some time figuring out our future with how to raise our daughter. We signed an agreement to always live within a twenty-mile radius of each other and that Casey would spend weekends with me.

I returned to Steamboat on New Year's Eve with great faith that all would work out. The next few months were a blur; maybe, it was the daily fresh snow storms that clouded my vision. My eyes definitely opened wide after taking my morning warm-up run on March 10. As I was racing down an expert trail, I launched off a jump. I successfully landed a 360, but there was a lady standing in a blind spot, applying her lipstick, and I collided with her. After an awkward violent hug, I realized she was badly injured. I called the ski patrol and watched her get taken away in an emergency sled.

My Irish guilt got the best of me; therefore, I skied to the patrol station at the bottom of the mountain, but she was already in an ambulance. "Please forgive me, God, I didn't mean to harm anyone." I prayed. I acknowledged to the ski patrol that I felt terrible for ruining the poor lady's vacation. The ski patrol took my ski pass away. To try and ease the pain, I sent flowers to the hospital.

Since I couldn't ski on my last day before departing home on March 17, St. Patrick's Day 1990, I decided to bungee jump out of a hot-air balloon. It made perfect sense at the time, plus bungee jumping was first on my bucket list.

Afterward, the girl that I was dating dropped me off at the airport, gave me a long hug, and said, "Now go home to your beautiful daughter and be the best father that you can be!"

I bought my first journal, boarded the plane, and wrote a letter to myself, including a bucket list. In summary, it read, "Dear PJ, get your act together, be the best father that you can be, and live life to its fullest." My bucket list consisted of many selfish adventures and risky thrills.

1. Bungee jumping (completed March 17, 1991)
2. Helicopter skiing in Alaska
3. Skydiving
4. Attend the Reggae Sunsplash in Jamaica
5. Travel Europe starting with Ireland
6. Finish college
7. Play golf at Pebble Beach
8. Attend the Reggae on the River
9. Attend the New Orleans Jazz festival
10. Attend as many Grateful Dead shows as possible
11. Ski Tuckerman's Ravine

Chapter 11

The Worst Two Weeks of My Life

IT ALL STARTED well with an amazing St. Patrick's celebration, parading around Holyoke with Casey. She was my Colleen.

After bringing Casey back to her mom's house, I received a phone call from the sheriff of Steamboat Springs, Colorado. I was charged with third-degree assault. The lady that I collided with decided to press charges for breaking her leg. I had to return to Steamboat and attend court that week.

The day after court, I helped my friend pack up his gear, and we planned to drive back to Holyoke together. The girl that I dated invited me to go to a wedding with her in Boulder, Colorado. It was a perfect plan, one last party with my girlfriend, then my Holyoke friend, Toby, would pick me up in Denver, and we would drive home.

The wedding had an open bar. After many drinks, we decided to keep the party going and went to see David Bowie in Denver. I had to trade-in my concert t-shirt for a blue jumpsuit that night. The Denver authorities pulled me over as I departed the parking lot; refusing the breathalyzer does not look good in Colorado.

It was a long ride back home to Holyoke. I was only home for a day when a good friend asked me to join him for a two-day business venture to Cape Cod. It was a good opportunity to make some money and help out a friend get his business ready for the summer.

After a sleepless night and a long day of work, we went to the beach for happy hour. For some reason, I decided to drive us back to our friend's house. Completely exhausted and distracted, I drove our car into a cranberry bog. I was arrested for reckless driving and spent another night in jail. That night, God shared the cell with me.

My dialogue with God was filled with shame and remorse. I asked for forgiveness for making him work so hard. I made my first covenant with God that consisted of completing my college degrees and providing a good life for Casey.

Chapter 12

Self-Discovery

WITH THREE DIFFERENT cases against me, I was in desperate need of a good lawyer. Once again, my mother called in a favor. This time, it was to her attorney. My driver's license was revoked for a year; therefore, I moved into my old bedroom at my mother's house and rode my bike to work every day at our new Holyoke Liquor Mart. As my brother Jerry and I learned about every aspect of running our own liquor store, I also learned about psychology at Holyoke Community College. It helped me understand myself.

Another worthy class was creative writing. I discovered my true voice within. Poetry came naturally to me. It granted me a way to convey the hidden divine meaning of life. After another friend died from an accident, God bless Mike P., I wrote:

Life's Friend

When a heartbeat that echoes love and friendship
dissipates into yesterday's wind,
Today loses a friend!
It is only when we listen to our own heartbeat
that we shall hear our loved one's again.

I turned the poem into a condolence card and gave it to the family. My journal began to fill up with meaningful words that captured the emotions of my journey.

Chapter 13

Little Brother, Grads, New Love, and Bucket List

THE YEAR 1991 was a year for new love. My dad and his new wife, Vicki, adopted a son named Alec. He was Vicki's only child and the love of her life; now the pressure was off me as the youngest son. More Shanahans, the merrier life became. Casey called him little Uncle Alec.

In late August of 1991, I met Tracy at a local Irish pub in Holyoke. She was visiting a couple of friends that I knew fairly well. Her friends gave her a friendly warning not to get involved with me because I already had a two-year-old daughter, and my pedigree wasn't too attractive at the time. She did not heed the warning; we continued our relationship throughout her senior year. I attended her graduation in May from Simmons College in Boston. The following weekend, she witnessed me graduate from Holyoke Community College. I graduated with honors and was nominated by faculty for the Green Key Honor Society. It was a proud moment for my parents to witness as well. All glory to God I knew in my heart.

Tracy and I were getting really close, even though she continued to live in Boston. She planned to get her master's from Boston University, and I transferred to UMass, Amherst, for my undergrad. She was aware of my bucket list; therefore, for my HCC graduation gift, she presented me with a gift certificate to go skydiving. I felt embarrassed at the time because I only gave her a card with an original PJ Poem written in it. Thank God for the Massachusetts Lottery.

Every night that I managed the Holyoke Liquor Mart, I played the lottery. My numbers were Casey's birthdate. On a normal Friday night in early June, my numbers won, granting me eleven thousand dollars. My Irish luck was obviously changing for the better. That weekend, Tracy witnessed me successfully jump out of an airplane in Northampton, Massachusetts.

During our celebratory dinner at Carmelina's Italian restaurant in Hadley, Massachusetts, I invited her to join me for one of my bucket list adventures. I presented her with a five-week Eurail Pass. She was completely surprised but genuinely concerned about me being away from Casey for that amount of time.

Before buying the Eurail Pass, CC granted me permission as long as I paid for Casey's first year at her preschool. The deal that I made with Casey was I had to bring her back a gift from every country I visited. Tracy and I had much to plan. We set the dates so we could travel and return home to attend our new universities in early September.

Planes, trains, and a ferry or two, a large backpack and new tent, plenty of cash, and a blank credit card should do. Oh yeah, my new passport too! Landing in Ireland for my first time was a dream come true. I've read and studied her majestic landscape, but to feel my feet on her green soil vibrated pure joy to my Irish heart. I felt the struggles of my ancestors, the love of the Irish poets, and tasted plenty of her beloved Guinness. Bed n Breakfast homes in Ireland welcomed us in their living rooms. It was pure heavenly hospitality. Even the Cliffs of Moher at the southwestern edge of the Burren region in County Clare greeted me personally. Her mighty winds captured my attention and forced my focus on the edge of a thousand-foot cliff; below there were Atlantic Ocean waves crashing on her walls. I drafted my ancient Celtic tale there.

I needed a way to share my love and admiration to all in Ireland; therefore, I took out my journal and began writing. "An old Celtic tradition began with a pen in a young Irish lad's hands from Holyoke. On these ancient majestic cliffs of Moher, take dried rose petals from a significant event and release them into the air. The strong winds from the Atlantic Ocean shall have her natural way of spreading love to all on the Emerald Isle. To witness the rose petals take flight is to promise eternal delight," Patrick John Shanahan, August 9, 1992.

By traveling from the Cliffs of Moher to West Galway to hear the Celtic tongue speak Gaelic brought many Irish poems that I read to reality. We were blessed to stay by the sea in Kinvara with friends from Holyoke. They knew the owners of the Kinvara Pub, and we were blessed to be invited to stay after the doors were locked one night. A young lad cleared off a table filled with empty pint glasses, then handed me a pair of wooden shoes. I accepted the offer; with my pint of Guinness gripped tightly in my Irish American hands, I jumped on top of the table with the wooden shoes on and did my best version of a jig. The band played instrumentally; therefore, I made up my own lyrics that many loved and sang along for a while. It was a true blessing for me to be part of the Irish entertainment that night. But leaving Ireland was a curse.

Departing Ireland with a two-week red beard, a pocketful of US currency, and a name like Patrick Shanahan raised some red flags when I arrived by ferry in Paris. As I went through customs in France, they split us up by gender. Tracy had no problems, but I was still intoxicated from partying with some new German friends all night, and the French custom agent was in a suspicious mood. He pulled me into a private interrogation room. The two-hour interrogation was in French until they brought an interpreter in. Tracy had no idea what was going on. They wanted to know who I really was and why I had so much cash on me. It was a nightmare. That was our first scare of the trip. Needless to say, we didn't stay in Paris for too long. Especially since no one would exchange my US currency because I didn't speak French.

We boarded a train for Amsterdam, knowing a friendly coffee shop would be happy to accept my US money. It was a therapeutic three days. We visited museums, coffee shops, and the famous Heineken brewery. From Amsterdam, we kept the party going in Munich, Germany. After too many steins of heavy German beers, we tried to rest our heads in a hostel that was an old circus tent. It was only ten dollars for the night, but we found out why. Upon entering the tent, they gave us an old potato sack and told us to go find a space to lay it on the dirt floor. That was our bed for the night. It should have been called a Hostile Tent, especially since circus music was our alarm clock at 7:00 a.m.

We actually crawled out of the tent, dragging our backpacks, vowing to never do that again. We traveled to Austria for a two-day peaceful, beautiful rehab. It was exactly what we needed to begin our journey to Italy. In Florence, romance was in the air and in our wine. We were falling in love. With each country visit, as I purchased a special gift fit for my beautiful little girl, Tracy began to comprehend my true love for my daughter. I was missing her dearly and had to explain the pain at some times. But I discovered that it's almost impossible for a nonparent to truly comprehend the love for a child.

Departing Italy by the shores of Brindisi, we traveled by ferry to Corfu, Greece. As we arrived at a private picturesque resort, the owner gathered a group of us, including new friends from Chicago. The owner gave us a concerning warning not to explore the nearby town because the working locals at the time were not appreciative of American tourists. He proceeded to offer all the amenities of his active resort, including an open bar, jet skis, cliff diving, tandem parasailing, and nude sunbathing. It proved to be a lethal combination of extreme fun, especially when we disobeyed his warning.

On the third day, after exhausting all of the fun that the resort offered, we overheard some of the resort employees talking about a Corfu native festival going on in town. The Chicago soccer boys, Tracy, and myself decided to go beyond our forbidden boundaries. I had to learn the rough way once again. We walked into a local drinking tradition that involved Greek music and clay plates smashed over your head as you drank ladles of a local favorite aperitif called ouzo. I was the only one that was naive enough to think the locals would welcome me in their drinking games. The welcome ended abruptly after the last plate was smashed over my head and I won.

As I stumbled out of the establishment, retreating toward our nearby beach resort, a few of the disgruntled, sore losers followed me on scooters. One of them had a lead pipe in his hand. Thank God my new Chicago friends were sober enough to realize what was about to happen. They were a minute too late but just in time to save my life! By the time they arrived on the scene, the violent act was already in motion. The locals hit me with the lead pipe in the back of my head as they drove by me on their scooters. Then they continued to kick me as I lay defenseless on the ground. By the time the Chicago boys arrived, I was a bloody mess, lying in the streets of Corfu.

When I awoke, Tracy was asking the owner of the resort if I was going to die. My blood-soaked shirt was on a table in front of me with barbaric instruments to stitch up my head. The owner, as he prepared to perform minor surgery with a fishing string thick enough to catch a shark, gave us his final warning. "You should leave Corfu before the gangs come back looking for you," he demanded.

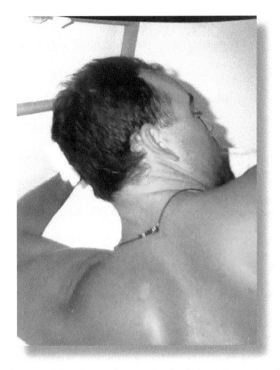

With a bruised body and a makeshift bandage on the back of my head, we boarded the ferry to return to Italy. Tracy was extremely concerned for my well-being; therefore, she called my mother and asked her if we should come home early. My mother, God bless her soul, said, "PJ has had many stitches and concussions. Keep it clean and enjoy the rest of the trip."

We rested and drank fine wine in Venice, Italy, for three days before we ventured to Switzerland to go whitewater rafting in Interlaken. With a plastic bag over the top of my head, I put a helmet over it and braced myself to take on the mighty rapids of the Lutschine. From the Eiger North Face of the Swiss Alps, we successfully challenged the class 4 rapids through Interlaken and, eventually, into the pristine waters of Lake Brienz. It was just what the doctor ordered to provide enough adrenaline to last for the end of the Euro trip.

The encore took place at the Notting Hill Carnival in London by surprise. We originally booked our trip to stay in the Notting Hill Gate district of London on August 30 and 31, before we flew back home on September 1. We arrived at our hotel early in the morning.

After a nice breakfast, we decided to go for a quiet walk around our new neighborhood. As we walked outside, we were greeted by hundreds of festively-dressed fun-loving people parading along, singing and dancing in the streets. It was the most amazing apropos ending for my Euro trip bucket list adventure. Live reggae bands played joyous uplifting music until the sun set at the end of the parade route.

On the plane ride home, I took out my journal, checked off the Europe trip on my bucket list, and documented many adventures. My only carry-on luggage was a backpack filled with cultural gifts representing each country that we visited for Casey Elizabeth Shanahan. I could barely wait to deliver her gifts and give her a big fatherly hug.

Chapter 14

Our New Liquor Store

I WAS BLESSED to take a five-week excursion because life was about to get busy. My mother proposed that my oldest brother, Jerry, and I run the new Holyoke Liquor Mart. Jerry would manage the mornings and all of the financials as I managed the evenings. In order to have a Saturday off, I had to work a double shift then take the following Saturday off. I scheduled my UMass courses around my career; therefore, I only registered for two classes per semester. I was in no rush to receive my undergrad degree because I planned to make my living running the liquor stores.

Tracy and I managed our relationship from a distance most days. She lived in Boston, and I moved into an apartment in Holyoke with my best friend, the "Doc." Casey lived with her mom but spent weekends with me when I wasn't working. Life resumed positive momentum.

One of the greatest positives for all of us Shanahans was when my beautiful cousin, Kara Shanahan, was crowned Colleen for the 1994 Holyoke St. Patrick's parade. I was blessed to witness and presented her with a dozen roses. Part of her Colleen blessing was a trip to Ireland; therefore, it was a perfect opportunity to share my "ancient Celtic tale" and tell my Uncle Billy to save the rose petals so they could release them into the winds at the Cliffs of Moher.

Working a family business had its positives. Our mother, God bless her, covered our schedule so Jerry, Chris, Laura, and I could attend Dead Shows together. As mentioned, The Dead concerts provided spiritual experiences that we missed from not going to church as a family.

Thank God I fulfilled my bucket list item because Jerry Garcia died on August 9, 1995. Before he died, I attended over two hundred

Grateful Dead concerts all over our beautiful country. My last concert was at the Knickerbocker Arena, Albany, New York, on June 22, 1995, and Jerry opened up with "Touch of Grey." "We will survive, I will get by." It was the same opener as the concert that I brought Casey too. Those lyrics continue to be a mantra for me. Thank you, Jerry!

Chapter 15

Reggae Sunsplash

I WAS IN need of another spiritual experience; therefore, I traveled to Jamaica by myself in August 1995. I planned my trip around a three-day reggae fest called Reggae Sunsplash. It was held in Kingston, the capital of Jamaica. The music began at sunset, and the last band ended at sunrise. I wanted to experience the Jamaican culture. I was a big fan of Bob Marley.

Before the festival started, I visited Bob's neighborhood called Trenchtown. I met a local Jamaican named Tony, who owned an old beat-up Camaro. He offered to be my private taxi for the weekend and gave me the real local tour. Tony had three young sons, and they lived in Shanty town, at least that's what he called it. I invited Tony to join me for the first night of the festival. He barely had enough money to feed his kids, so I told him I would take care of all the expenses and buy gas. He gratefully accepted.

We had an amazing time together. After Gregory Issacs brought the sun up, Tony wanted to introduce me to his kids. He warned me that I would probably be the only white person in his neighborhood, but I would be safe as long as I was with him.

As we drove into the district at 7:30 a.m., some neighborhood friends of his were chasing after a rude boy with sticks in their hands. Tony began speaking Patois, his local language, out of his window. I could barely comprehend what they were talking about, but it was easy enough to figure out the angry energy. The rude boy they were chasing robbed an elderly lady from the neighborhood.

Tony told me to hold on as he sped up and chased after the guy in the Camaro. The adrenaline was stronger than any Jamaican coffee that I needed at that time in the morning, especially, after being up all night. Tony caught up to the rude boy and forced him into an alleyway. As the rude boy climbed over a fence, Tony reached in the back seat, grabbed a machete, and jumped out of the car. By this time, the other neighborhood friends caught up to us.

I initially stayed in the car, but the suspense and the curiosity of witnessing neighborhood Jamaican justice got the best of me. I climbed on top of a little tin shack and watched how they handled thieves in their neighborhood. All I can say is there was no need to call the police. That rude boy would never steal again. Tony walked back to the car with the elderly lady's purse, and the only thing he said was, "Sorry you had to witness that."

We drove in silence to his nearby tin roof humble home. Chickens ran around his small yard, and a couple of goats roamed about. As we walked into his house, he forewarned his wife that he had a guest with him. She was surprised but extremely welcoming. There was no flooring, only dirt, and his three young sons slept in the same bed. Tony was proud to introduce them to me. I was blessed to meet them all. I gave his wife some money to go to the local farmers market and answered many curious questions from his sons while we waited for her to return.

She returned with a basket of native fruits that I never heard of until that morning. We all sat outside in the early morning sunshine, eating guanabio, jackfruit, and coolie plums. Tony knew that I was exhausted, so he told his kids that Mr. PJ had to go get some sleep and prepare for another night of great reggae music.

The rest of the festival was filled with fun, great reggae music, and awesome food. Tony and I exchanged letters a few times that year. Reggae Sunsplash, Kingston Style, will always remain in my heart's memory.

Chapter 16

The Proposal

TRACY FINISHED HER master's from Boston University the following spring. We decided to move in together in Northampton, Massachusetts. After a year of living together and learning to trust our relationship, I had an engagement ring made with the help from my mother's little purple Crown Royal bag of mismatched diamonds. She had one beautiful diamond earring that belonged to her mother, Alice, that I chose to transform into a gorgeous engagement ring.

I planned to propose on Christmas Eve after I closed the liquor store. We had a reservation for our intimate traditional annual meal at the Delaney House. But after locking the liquor store doors on December 23, I took the ring out of our safe and prayed in the darkness. I made a deal with God; if I set the alarm successfully in the dark, then I would propose after midnight. The alarm was set; now I had to change my game plan on the way home. With an unshaven face, wine on my breath, tired from a long, busy day, I woke Tracy up at 12:05 a.m.; It was officially Christmas Eve. I told her my original plan and my deal with God, then I got on my knees and proposed to her. Basically, I shared that most days, I will be unshaven, working hard to make a good living for us, and will always be filled with spontaneous love for her. She gratefully accepted, and we decided to walk over to an Irish Pub that my friend Joe managed. After sharing our news, he bought us a bottle of fine champagne, wished us much love and a Merry Christmas. Our Christmas season was blessed with promise. We left our wedding date open.

Chapter 17

New Orleans Jazz Fest

SINCE MY UMASS graduation date was off in the distance, I decided to check off another festival on my bucket list. In 1996, I attended the famous New Orleans Jazz Festival with a few of my best friends. It filled the void with no Dead shows to attend and overflowed into the year; therefore, I decided to make it an annual.

The following year, I invited Tracy at the risk of our engagement. The New Orleans festival was a huge party that began during the day and could possibly extend into the next morning. I packed my own suitcase and stuffed my socks with party favors. The festival had two options, the last weekend of April or the first weekend of May. We chose the second because it began on Thursday and ended Sunday night for most people.

It was a long festive weekend. On Sunday, the closing day, the entire festival marched out of the race track and headed straight to Bourbon Street. Tracy was showing signs of intoxication but tried to keep up. We followed the energy in and out of different clubs around the French Quarter as the clock continued its cycle. Our hotel was in the French Quarter; eventually, the energy would guide us to bed.

In one of the jazz clubs, I overheard a few locals promoting the very last act of the festival weekend. Walter "Wolfman" Washington was playing at the Maple Leaf Club outside the French Quarter beginning at 2:00 a.m. It was 10:30 p.m.; our flight home was at 8:30 a.m. Monday morning. As we were walking toward our hotel, I rehearsed my plan in my head, then delivered my proposal.

"Let's go back to our room, pack our suitcases, and make passionate N'Orleans love," I suggested.

She laughed at me and said, "You are on your own with the passionate love because I'm all done!"

That's exactly what I wanted to hear. "Okay, I understand. I'll pack my gear, then I'm going to see the final act of the festival weekend. You get enough sleep for the both of us. I'll have a taxi waiting for us in the morning and will bring you breakfast," I told her. She called me crazy as I walked out the door.

I wasn't the only crazy one; the Maple Leaf club was packed. They had a crawfish boil going on in the side alley. A bowl of the New Orleans finest ingredients, with a local Abita Amber, was the perfect recipe to keep the positive energy going. As I was working my way toward the front of the stage, another festival rebel walked past me and grabbed a piece of my cornbread. I threw a crawfish at him, hit him in the back of the head, and said, "Yo, there are no drive-thrus in New Orleans."

He turned around with a puzzled look, hugged me, and screamed, "You're alive!"

Truth be told, we didn't recognize each other at first glance. My U of Tampa friend recognized my raspy voice. Buddha was the first Dead Head that I met back in 1985 at college. We haven't seen each other since then. When he was at a Grateful Dead concert in 1994 at the Oakland Coliseum, he was handed a black-and-white photo with the name Patrick Shanahan on it that resembled me. It read, "Patrick Shanahan overdosed at a Dead Show, if anyone knows him, please contact the police." Buddha thought I died and actually had a candle burning ceremony for me.

I was resurrected at 3:00 a.m., New Orleans 1997, at least in his mind. We danced and laughed until the sun came up, then he drove Tracy and I to the airport. I tried to explain to Tracy on the way, but she was a little annoyed at me; a silent treatment was my invite to sleep all the way back home.

Chapter 18

Wedding Plans, God's Plan

WHEN THE SILENT treatment was finally lifted, my fiancée spoke clearly. "You don't know when to stop, do you?" she asked in a concerned tone. It was a good question, but I always had a good answer when the subject was about my partying. I responded to her question with a spiritual question.

"If I stopped and never went to the Maple Leaf Club, Buddha would still think that I was dead. Is that what you want friends to be thinking about me?" That changed the subject quickly and had me thinking more deeply about what motivates me. Was it the alcohol, the music, the thrill of life? Or was it God?

What direction shall I go? I began to ask God each morning when I woke up. It became part of my meditation practice. It was good timing because we had some important future plans to agree on. My thirtieth birthday was approaching in September, and most importantly, we needed to confirm wedding dates.

As Memorial weekend was approaching, so was another opportunity to add an adventure to my bucket list. The liquor stores were closed on Memorial Day, Monday. Because the store was always closed on the Sabbath, that provided a three-day weekend for us. I always wanted to hike and ski Tuckerman Ravine in New Hampshire. Tuckerman Ravine is a glacial cirque on the southwest face of the highest mountain in New England. Mt. Washington, if the winter provided enough snow, enticed many adventurous skiers to hike her ravine and ski down in late spring. There was plenty of good snow left to enjoy from the winter of 1997. Now I just had to entice Tracy to travel with me again.

Since Tracy rejected my idea of getting married on the Cliffs of Moher in Ireland, we compromised with having part of our reception near the cliffs in Ogunquit, Maine. They were absolutely stunning, and we loved to visit there. After a morning meditation, the Memorial weekend plans were drafted; it read: hike and ski Tuckerman Ravine in New Hampshire, camp out, then travel in the morning to the coast of Maine to plan our wedding. Tracy liked the plan, except the dangerous skiing part and the camping with the spring bugs. I was learning more about my fiancée's comfort zone.

The weekend worked out beautifully. It was a gorgeous spring sunny weekend with comfortable temperatures at night to keep the bugs away and encouraged snuggling for warmth. Hiking two miles up to the ravine with ski gear in a backpack provided plenty of healthy exercise. At the base of the ravine, the scene resembled a beach party. Many other girls joined Tracy as she sunbathed on the rocks while I climbed another thousand feet to the peak of the ravine with cousin Bob Dillon and his son Josh. The views were breathtaking, but the steep skiing on late spring snow filled my lungs with exhilaration. After hiking the peak three times, I had just enough energy with plenty of gratitude to descend to our camping area.

A starlit evening set the mood, but the bottle of fine Pinot Noir wine opened the door to our tent for an intimate night of love. We exited New Hampshire with refreshed excitement to plan our future. Even though we had vacationed in Ogunquit, Maine, a few times, it felt like we were discovering her beauty for the first time. We found the perfect reception restaurant off the beaten path hidden in the woods called the Clay Hill Farms. They had a serene sanctuary area to walk around and witness Mother Nature, an outdoor deck for the happy hour, and a tasty menu. It was quaint and could accommodate our party on the Sunday of Memorial weekend 1999.

We chose Memorial weekend because we wanted a two-day celebration with immediate family and significant others. The morning after our wedding, we planned a jazz brunch at the Cliff House resort and booked our honeymoon suite. Our room had a large balcony looking out East into the Atlantic Ocean. It was perfect for early morning sunrise. We found a comfortable family-owned small hotel with a nice outdoor heated pool to accommodate all of our guests for two nights. Now, we needed to find a Catholic Church in town. I tried convincing Tracy to get married on the Cliffside of Cape Neddick, Maine, but she was adamant about getting married in a Catholic Church.

The timing was divine; there was a 4:00 p.m. Mass at a local Catholic church. It was 3:30 p.m., which allowed no time to change; therefore, we walked into Mass with our flip-flops on, wearing our finest beach gear. It was a small church called St. Mary's near the beach. It looked welcoming and promising to have our wedding vows take place within her sandstone divine walls. Truth be told, for some reason, it felt foreign to me as I walked through the doors as the church bells were ringing. The service was longer than I remember, with many songs that I did not know the words to. I continued to feel out of place, then it really got awkward.

It was finally time to receive communion. In a Catholic Church, the Holy Eucharist is the most important of the seven sacraments. I made my first communion in second grade and have practiced the sacrament many times since. As mentioned, it was a long Mass already, and the line for communion appeared to be the length of a football field. I saw an open lane toward a Eucharist minister, hiding by himself in the corner of the church. I was surprised that no one was going to him. I left my formation and walked quickly toward him. As I approached him, he was prepared and extended the chalice towards me. He had me confused immediately; back home, the Eucharistic minister usually hands you the communion, not the chalice. I reached my hands out palms up, but he continued to offer me the chalice. I was completely baffled, so I put my fingers in, thinking it was the "help yourself communion lane," and that's when the nice man almost fainted. I felt liquid and even more confused. I blessed myself, thinking it was holy water. Tracy and the whole church heard the man yell, "You can't put your fingers in the holy wine, the blood of Christ is sacred!" With God's blood dripping off my forehead, I sprinted for my end zone in the parking lot.

By the time Tracy came out, I was already in my convertible Saab with the top down. She was still hysterically laughing at me. "It looks like you are not interested in asking the church about getting married there?" She asked the question knowing the answer already.

"Oh well, I guess we have to get married on the cliffs because that church will definitely not forgive me for contaminating the holy wine," I responded with a smirk on my face.

It was time to regroup back at our beachside campground. As we were driving along the majestic rocky shores of Maine with the convertible top down, I sensed a mood change in Tracy; therefore, I needed to keep our spirits high. I began to silently ask God what his plan was for us. Within the next mile, I saw a lobsterman setting up shop along the shore. He had four ten-gallon pots, four small open fires going set upon rocks, and a couple of large coolers. I immediately pulled over without warning Tracy. The quick stop and the sight of the Maine lobsterman snapped her back into the present moment. "Thank you, God!" I yelled joyfully.

We were the local lobsterman's first customer. He boiled us three three-pound fresh lobsters, shared a story or two, and set the mood for more adventure. Tracy and I returned to our campsite excited for a romantic feast by the sea. An open fire, plenty of tasty lobster, and some good Chardonnay created hopeful conversation. We fell asleep that evening with faith that our wedding plans would work out the way God wanted it to.

Chapter 19

Sacred Heart as God's Plan

WHEN WE RETURNED home, we still had no church to call our own, so I called my mother. I shared our adventure and my embarrassment about the holy wine. She responded by inviting us to her new church in Springfield, Massachusetts, called Sacred Heart. "You will love Father Farland, he is very welcoming, he has a short mass with a joke, right up your alley, son." My mother concluded. The very next Sunday, Tracy and I attended Mass and loved the homily, especially the joke. The first joke I heard him tell was about an indirect confession, forgiveness, and adultery.

> Patrick walked into Mass, planning to steal a new hat because he lost his favorite one. The nuns spotted him and dragged him up in front of the priest. He was forced to listen to the sermon. After Mass, Patrick thanked the priest, confessed that he planned to steal a new hat, but truly thanked him for reminding him of where he lost his. The priest responded, "You are forgiven, Patrick, but how did I remind you of where you lost yours?"
>
> Patrick said, "When you were preaching about adultery, I remembered where I left mine."

I was cracking up while Tracy was trying to figure out what was so funny. We met with Father Farland after Mass, and he encouraged us to join Sacred Heart Church. It was the first time that I truly felt comfortable in a church since Holy Cross. I was hoping that Tracy felt the same way. Father Farland checked his schedule, and sure enough he had Sunday Memorial weekend 1999 open. God was unveiling his plan for us.

We planned our wedding time, set the date, and agreed on inviting our friends to the church ceremony. After a tailgate party in the parking lot, we would travel in a convoy with immediate family to the Clay Hill Farm for our reception dinner.

Chapter 20

The Divine Plan

I HAD COMPLETED all of my communication courses for my undergrad degree at UMass but still had some credits to fulfill. The liquor store kept me busy at night, but my schedule allowed me to be productive during the days. We had some nitty-gritty details to take care of in order to attain a marriage license. Part of it was a full physical evaluation, including blood work.

At that stage in my life, I thought I was in good shape. I swam for exercise, drank plenty of red wine at night, and slept well. I remember the phone call from my doctor after my blood work was completed.

Doctor Bob, our family doctor, married my cousin. We were close, and he was personally invested in my well-being. He sounded concerned on the phone, requested a meeting to discuss the results, and asked me how my wedding plans were going. I responded to his concerned tone, "Thank you, Bob, plans are going well, but you have me worried now. Our meeting is many hours away. Can you please let me know why you sound concerned?"

He said, "You have high iron counts in your liver, and it looks like hemochromatosis, but we need to do more tests."

"What the hell is hemoscoliosis?" I asked.

He laughed at my pronunciation and told me that it's hereditary but treatable. I wish I didn't ask. "It" sounded intimidating. I looked it up while I was working at the liquor store that night. Trying to decipher the medical jargon created anxiety; therefore, I opened a nice bottle of Pinot Noir.

The drive to my doctor's office in the morning was only ten minutes. The speed limit was 30 mph, but my mind was racing at least forty miles per minute. Thank God I didn't have to wait long when I arrived.

"Good morning, PJ," Bob said.

"I sure hope so, Bob, what is hemo blah blah blah, and how serious is it?"

He told me that it's hereditary but can't find any history of it in our family but is concerned because both of my grandfathers died in their early forties. It led to a long intriguing conversation about how my grandfathers passed away. The short of it is, I found out that both of my grandfathers were alcoholic and died from heart complications. As mentioned, I never met them and only knew of their accomplishments during their short lives. Alcoholism was a well-kept secret in our family.

It was a humbling meeting. I learned that hemochromatosis is a genetic disorder characterized by excessive intestinal absorption of dietary iron that stores in the liver, disrupting normal function. Dr. Bob's theory was that it was possible that both of my grandfathers had it, but since the diagnosis of it wasn't truly discovered until 1976, he couldn't confirm that. What he did confirm captured my attention. "HC" was highly diagnosed in the Irish population.

"Wow, is it treatable?" I asked with hope in my heart and liver.

"Yes, but it will take some time and some life adjustments. You will need to have phlebotomies and will have to quit drinking," he responded seriously.

"What the hell are bottomies?" I asked, ignoring the part of quitting drinking. He told me that I would have to give blood every month, but that was only a Band-Aid, then proceeded to inquire about my drinking. That was the longest part of our discussion and was the first time that I was medically confronted about my alcohol consumption.

I drove around most of the morning, with my top down cranking some Grateful Dead, ignoring the reality that I had to quit drinking and that my career was running liquor stores. It really didn't hit me until 7:00 p.m. when I was restocking the red wine section of the Holyoke Liquor Mart. I wanted to open every bottle. It was a long, restless night. I didn't tell Tracy about my results until she asked me during breakfast. She had way too many questions, concerns, and worries for me to digest; I focused on my strong coffee and again tried ignoring the challenge of not drinking.

I tried to prove to myself and my fiancée that it was no big deal for the next few months. My career was haunting me and so were all of the bottles in the liquor store, even the little nips. One particularly hot summer night, I really wanted a cold beer to wash down my dinner as I was taking a break in my office. I decided that one wasn't going to kill me. That night, I closed an Irish Pub in town and drove home drunk again. Before I got out of my car, I took a long look in my "rearview" mirror. It was there that I saw my past troubles, especially obvious was my fake front tooth.

In eighth grade on Veteran's Day, a day off from school, a few of my friends and I spent the day drinking Wild Irish Rose and warm 16 oz. Miller Beer, "the high life" of beers. We stumbled out of the woods and into a nearby neighborhood. After my friend stumbled into a trash can and knocked it over, we were violently chased by the owner of the house who was wearing fatigues. The last thing I remember was running down the steep paved Bemis road. Then I woke up in a hospital with my mother and a nurse asking me how much and what kind of alcohol I drank. If my memory serves me well, that was truly the first time that I lied about my drinking.

I broke my front tooth that day in eighth grade because of my drinking and ignored it ever since. I never told Tracy the truth about my fake tooth, but I was about to.

Tracy was awake as usual, worried about me as I stumbled in the doors at 2:30 a.m. She knew the liquor store closed at 11:00 p.m. I began the conversation with, "I have a confession." Then I launched into my story of my broken tooth.

We both agreed that I needed help. The next day, I called my sober uncle and inquired about how he stayed sober. He introduced me to Alcoholics Anonymous. It was definitely contradicting and challenging going to AA meetings during the day then working at our liquor store at night. But one day at a time, anything is possible, especially with Jesus as my higher power.

I celebrated my first sober New Year's Eve that year. The AA program reintroduced prayers into my life and daily miracles happened. One minute after I opened the liquor store on a Saturday morning, a regular customer that I called Nickels—because he was always short a nickel—walked in and asked me if I would attend his funeral on Sunday. He was a shaky mess and needed his morning medicine. "One nip of vodka will do the trick," he said.

"What about the rest of the day?" I asked sarcastically. Then I caught myself, apologized immediately, and invited him into my office.

I gave him two nips of cheap vodka to calm his nerves then proceeded to ask him about his funeral. He admitted that he has been an alcoholic for many years and felt like death. Within the next half hour, I shared my story and provided hope. I encouraged him to allow me to drive him to a detox facility. It was an interesting start to my Saturday double shift at the Holyoke Liquor Mart.

Later that day, a high school friend of mine came into the store to buy a bottle of wine. She asked me how college was going. I told her that I only needed six more credits and was trying to figure out what courses to take. She was a director at a local high school for behavioral kids. As the conversation progressed, she offered me an intern position as a school counselor. I could earn my six credits, earn twelve dollars per hour, and graduate from UMass.

Three miracles took place on my first sober double shift at the Holyoke Liquor Mart. First and most important, I stayed sober; second, I was able to help another alcoholic; and third, I received a blessing from an old high school friend who knew all about my shenanigans back in the '80s. Her thought process was it takes a recovered behavioral student to help a struggling one. That thought created many thoughts for me to meditate on.

I was excited to share my new plan with my fiancée and my UMass advisor. There were thousands of communication majors at UMass, and I knew that I would remain anonymous if I didn't get to know my advisor. I walked into his office without an appointment early Monday morning, with an extra coffee in my hand. After introducing myself, he stood up and cheerfully said, "Oh my god, Patrick Shanahan, you are at the top of my list to call today and discuss a plan for your last six credits."

I responded, "Our God, don't be selfish. He likes to share his grace." We spent the next hour truly getting to know each other. We talked more about life and less about school since I already had a plan.

I told him that I wasn't in a rush to graduate, and after he stopped laughing, he responded, "Obviously, you graduated from high school in 1985."

"How about we stretch this out until the May 22, 1999, graduation, then I can give my diploma to my wife for a wedding gift?" I asked him between laughs.

"That sounds perfect, and by the way, my daughter is getting married that same weekend." He joyfully shared. We gave each other cheers with our empty coffee cups. He gratefully signed the papers for my intern, then we set monthly meetings to discuss my experiences.

Chapter 21

The Eye Opener

THANK GOD FOR sobriety because I took on a busy schedule that year. I worked as a crisis educational counselor at the Poet Seat School in Greenfield, Massachusetts, from 8:30 a.m. until 2:00 p.m. each day and managed the liquor store from 3:00 p.m. until 11:00 p.m. each night. I kept the Sabbath day holy by attending Mass at Sacred Heart Church and shared quality time with Casey and Tracy. I had monthly phlebotomies scheduled to help care for my hemochromatosis, but most importantly, I attended the daily 7:00 a.m. "Eye Opener" AA meeting to learn more about my disease called alcoholism.

Daily recovery was a humbling experience for me. I met some amazing people that helped me on my journey. On the other hand, my siblings became concerned because both hemochromatosis and alcoholism were hereditary. My new diagnoses forced them to look at their lives, but initially, they acted as if I was contagious. I had to remind them, with a sense of humor, that I was the third son; therefore, I was not the original carrier of this newly discovered disease.

Their concern enticed me to inquire about my grandfathers' early-age deaths. I found out that Jerome Shanahan knew and accepted his alcoholism. He was eight years sober when he had a heart attack in his living room at the age of forty-two. He used to host AA meetings at his house. But Larry Gobeille, who originally operated our family liquor business, struggled with alcoholism and possibly died because of his denial. As mentioned, it remains uncertain if they had hemochromatosis. The known facts were enough to keep me sober on a daily basis.

Chapter 22

Graduation

APPROACHING GRADUATION IN 1999, fourteen years since my 1985 high school grad, was an exciting time for me. It almost created as much adrenaline as bungee jumping and skydiving. College graduation was on my bucket list. UMass commencement took place in the football stadium with thousands of graduates. My parents attended separately and were curious how they would witness me in the massive crowd. I told them not to worry, that I would figure it out.

I drove my convertible to commencement by myself. As I went into my trunk to retrieve my cap and gown, I found an old Father's Day card from Casey that was shaped as a big round yellow smiley face and, on the back of it, in her handwriting, said, "I am happy that you are my daddy." I took a shoelace from my golf shoes, poked a hole in the big round card, and wore it like "bling." Also in my trunk was a rainbow-colored umbrella hat that was a perfect replacement for my traditional graduation cap. A promise is a promise. I told my parents that I would figure out how they would locate me.

It was a memorable experience for all of us. As the graduates around me were enjoying bottles of champagne, I was busy thanking God. Now it was time to focus on our wedding.

Chapter 23

The Wedding and Sober Honeymoon

MAY 30, 1999, was a beautiful sunny Sunday. Father Farland provided a joyful ceremony. Casey was our flower girl, and her mother attended our wedding, supporting us with loving respect. Tracy's brother was my best man, but I also had many great friends there to cheer us on. They provided enough cheer to turn a sober tailgate party into a memorable festival. As planned, only immediate family and their significant others joined our convoy for the two-hour drive to Ogunquit, Maine.

As we arrived at the Clay Hill Farm, our gracious hostess showed Tracy her bridal powder room. Before we booked our reception, they warned us that there was another wedding taking place on premise. We had our own reception space, but the brides shared the powder room. When Tracy and the other gorgeous bride exited, it provided a perfect picture. I asked permission to take the photo of both brides, and my voice startled the other bride's father.

My UMass advisor turned around, quickly yelling, "Shanahan, I thought I got rid of you. Are you crashing my daughter's wedding?" Only God could orchestrate such a divine surprise like that. We never exchanged personal details of our weddings. It was a spiritual encounter for all.

The reception was flawless and fun, but the jazz brunch the next morning on the cliffs of Maine was amazing. My favorite was waking up early in our honeymoon suite to witness our first sunrise as a married couple. Then we all enjoyed the sunny views of the majestic Atlantic Ocean. We filled our bellies and digested to a relaxing live Jazz band. The women had spa treatments scheduled for after, and most of us guys played golf at Cape Neddick Country Club.

It was just the beginning of many majestic sunrises and ocean view golf rounds. Our real two-week honeymoon was on the US Virgin Island of St. Croix. Point Udall on St Croix was the farthest east location in the United States Virgin Islands; therefore, we witnessed many brilliant beginnings of our new life together. As a bonus, the Carambola Resort that we stayed at had the top-rated golf course to play in all of the US Virgin Islands.

Most mornings, after sunrise, I played golf as Tracy enjoyed private yoga sessions on Carambola Beach. One morning, I decided to join Tracy for a cliff climb hike with her private yoga instructor. As we were ascending the steep cliffs, the yoga instructor looked back to check on me.

"Are you okay back there?" She asked me between laughs.

"One step at a time. I'll be fine," I responded.

When we finally reached the peak, we could see St. John across the mesmerizing azure blue waters of the Caribbean Sea. The heavenly views provided many picturesque photos but also invited us to converse on a spiritual level. The instructor picked up on my one-step-at-a-time comment and asked me if I was a friend of Bill W. That was a tactful anonymous way of asking if I was in the AA program of recovery. Bill Wilson was one of the founders of Alcoholics Anonymous.

In the program, it is known, where there are two or more recovering alcoholics, that's enough to have an AA meeting. Tracy's eyes rolled, head nodded, and said, "Here we go again with PJ's spiritual encounters." It was a memorable meeting that led to an invite to be her guest speaker at the S.t Croix Christiansted AA group. The most divine part was the meeting was held in the Holy Cross Catholic Church. Once again, only God could orchestrate the divinity that was happening in my life.

Chapter 24

The Knoll Cabin

THE HONEYMOON WAS over, but summer was about to begin. I finished up the school year as a crisis counselor on a positive note. The Poet Seat School triggered many emotions that fulfilled my heart's purpose. On the other hand, the liquor business drained me and continued to test my sobriety.

I had many intimate conversations with God on my rides home after closing the store. My family needed me to manage our new Holyoke Liquor Mart at night, and it provided a stable financial future for us, but was it worth my life?

The Eye Opener AA meeting was a perfect setting to discuss my conflict. Obviously, the other alcoholics strongly persuaded me to think of my sobriety. I discussed my scenario on a deeper level with my sponsor, who was my uncle at the time. He suggested that I go on a retreat to Temenos. It was a nearby sanctuary that rented solo self-sufficient cabins in the silent woods on Mt. Mineral, Shutesbury, Massachusetts. He assured me that a three-day silent retreat would provide the answers for my inner conflict.

There was no suitcase needed, just the "essentials" he suggested. I laughed at his choice of words. But sure enough, the weekend that I booked began with strong, windy rain. During the one-mile ascent to the Knoll Cabin, all that I could think of was my U of Tampa room-mate's swimming goggles. It had me laughing all the way through the dark woods and cleansed me with karmic energy.

I was completely drenched by the time I found the hidden treasure called the Knoll. There was no check-in required. I mailed a check a week before and was instructed to leave the cabin the way I found it. It was far from the Carambola Resort, but as I loaded the wood-burning stove, the warmth and fresh smell of local dried oak caressed my soul.

The first night of my silent retreat was noisy with many thoughts. Throughout the night, I woke from many mini dreams that all had similar themes of past experiences. Stoking the fire brought peace and invited me back to the extreme presence. It was there and then that I truly learned what meditation was all about.

All alone but filled with God's grace, I learned to listen to my immediate surroundings and less of my turbulent thoughts. The Knoll Cabin itself became my comforter. Her serene silence enveloped my life.

I found the cabin's journal that my uncle told me about and began writing.

> The rain has cleansed my past, her damp chill forced the presence, it is here, now, always available, everything I truly need, my authentic self. (PJ 1999)

The second day I walked the ancient paths of Mt. Mineral, listening to all that needed to be heard in the present moment. It was a divine orchestra directed by God and Mother Nature. I sat by a patient stream and repeated a new poem that I wrote in the presence of God.

> The patient stream continuously flows with faith as it approaches its destiny of eternal serenity. (PJ 1999)

That second evening in the Knoll Cabin revealed my future path. My friend's comment, "It takes a recovered behavioral student to help out a struggling one," echoed in the silence. My past academic failures became my strengths in my mind. My intern position for six credits created embers in my soul, and I wanted to keep that fire going. It also became clear that God intervened by introducing hemochromatosis in my life. He needed me sober at that stage in life to be of some use to him.

I woke up the last morning on Mt. Mineral, figuratively and literally, by drafting my blueprints for my future. It looked promising, but I knew I needed a master's in educational psychology in order to make a decent living as a counselor. Most importantly, I needed to let my family know that I had to leave the liquor business to save my life.

In a whispering state of being, I felt like I tiptoed out of the Knoll Cabin. I wanted to leave it as peacefully as I found it for the next retreatant. My gear felt lighter on the descent off the mountain, until I realized it was my mind. Everything was silent; the world and the trees that occupied it were still. I wanted to preserve that feeling for as long as I could, but I knew, once I returned to society, the noise would return. It would be up to me to create my daily silence; therefore, I vowed to practice meditation on a daily basis.

Chapter 25

Cum Laude

THE ARRIVAL BACK home greeted me with the most important piece of mail. The mailman just arrived as I was walking to my front door. He had one piece that I had to sign for. It had a UMass emblem on it. Because our commencement had thousands of graduates, we did not receive our diplomas. I tore it open with great anticipation and discovered my ticket for my future.

My diploma from UMass came with a gold sticker and a red ribbon reading cum laude on it. I never truly paid attention to my grades at UMass. I enjoyed all of my classes so much that the grades took care of themselves. I knew that those two Latin words printed on my diploma would open many doors for a master's program in educational psychology.

No better time than the present, I thought. I made myself a green tea and researched master programs in the local area. American International College in Springfield, Massachusetts, captured my attention. I filled out an application online, made an appointment for an interview, and confirmed a tour of campus for the upcoming week.

Knowing that a master's would take at least two years, I decided to hold off on sharing my future plans with my family until the end of summer. Most urgent was sharing my new plan with my new wife. I prayed that she would support the plan and handed the rest over to God.

During my tour on the AIC campus, I kept noticing a want ad posted on bulletin boards across the campus. They were like big red stop signs, but the tour guide kept a steady pace. Finally, at the end of my tour, I stopped and read what was capturing my attention.

American International College had a small building on campus called the Curtis Blake Center. Curtis Blake was one of the original founders of the Friendly Ice Cream Corporation, and he was a Springfield, Massachusetts, resident. Later in his life, Mr. Blake discovered that he was dyslexic and decided to fund a program that tested and provided special education for local families with dyslexia. They had a small school at a different location that was looking for a counselor for the upcoming school year.

"No better time than the present" became my new mantra. I walked into the Curtis Blake Center that afternoon and walked out an hour later with a new job. *All glory to God*, I chanted all the way home.

Chapter 26

Confession Time

AS AN IRISH Catholic, the guilt of my newfound future plans began to weigh heavy on my heart. I knew that my mother planned on my brother and I owning the stores in the future. All of my dishonest behaviors while working at our stores haunted me, especially when I stole a book of lottery tickets, banking on winning a million dollars. It was a book of three hundred one-dollar scratch tickets, and I only won ninety dollars. My original plan was to win big and pay back the three hundred dollars. I had to cash in the winning tickets at different stores so I wouldn't get caught, but my mother reported the book missing to the state lottery agent. Since the tickets had codes on the back of them, one of the convenience stores conveniently took down my license plate and reported it to the police. The police called my mother and asked her if she recognized the plate number. It was the most embarrassing and degrading sin of my life. It haunted me more than lying about my new gloves I received from Christmas and stealing a cemetery log for a Mother's Day gift.

Before I shared my new future plans with my mom, I needed to beg for forgiveness from my past. On a random midweek day, I called Father Farland and asked him if he would grant me a confession. He gracefully invited me to attend a confession before the 5:00 p.m. weekly Mass. My last formal Catholic confession was my only one, and it was to fulfill requirements to be confirmed to Catholicism back in tenth grade.

Father Farland greeted me with a suspicious smile, at least in my mind. We spent a good hour together. As I was walking out of the confessional booth, my mother walked into Church. *Wow*, I thought, *God works quick*. Her smile was more suspicious than Father Farland. We sat, kneeled, and stood in prayer together for the entire Mass. After Mass, I took my mother out for dinner and shared my future plans. It was a humbling meal.

Chapter 27

History

I MADE HISTORY working at the Curtis Blake School. I was the only male. It was a blessing to work with all women. Thank God my mother was my boss for many years. That wasn't the only blessing; because I technically worked for the college, my master's was paid for.

Nothing comes for free. The hardest and most emotional day of counseling was on September 11, 2001. I was in charge of gathering all of our students together in the auditorium. There were no classes that taught me how to deal with such a tragedy like 9/11. God placed me where I was supposed to be that day, and he guided all of my actions. I learned more on September 11, 2001, than I did in all of my psychology classes combined. The most valuable lesson was to always trust God.

After managing that crisis, the school began to trust my counseling and granted me permission to offer an after-school social-emotional program. The success of that program led to my summer adventure program.

I designed a week-long adventure program and proposed it to the director of the Curtis Blake School. He loved the idea. I was paid to do all of my favorite summer activities with students: kayaking, cliff diving, hiking, and many other impromptu activities. I taught them how to evaluate risk and introduced challenges by choice. We had an amazing week; my first summer adventure camp was a success.

Chapter 28

Special Year

THE YEAR 2002 was a special year, especially when the Patriots beat the Rams in New Orleans, with Tom Brady as their quarterback. My brothers Jerry and Chris attended the game. They claim that it was because of them that the Patriots won.

Then in May, I received my master's in educational psychology and became a licensed counselor. I made history once again, but this time, it was because I was the first Shanahan to receive a master's degree. The academic accolades became my new high; therefore, I enrolled to continue my education even further. I set my next goal to receive a certificate of an advanced graduate degree.

In July, I was honored to be the tournament poet for a family that I grew up with in the Highlands. Their brother Tom died, and they had an annual fundraising golf tournament. It was the first of many memorials that I wrote for.

Thank You

Each conscious breath
Creates a celebration;
For granted
We may breathe
Until we inhale with gratitude
Then we shall receive
The treasure hidden in each precious moment.
As the day unfolds
Listen to the laughter
Shared from soul to soul;
Hear with your heart

All the stories told.
"Thank you, Tom Hoey, for all of your memories,"
Gratefully, Patrick J. Shanahan

Between working every day and taking intense psychology classes at night, life was moving along, until September 29, 2003; our beloved uncle Neal Shanahan suddenly died at the age of sixty-one in Vale, San Diego. Neal moved to the Black Hills after retiring from teaching in Alaska. The day he died, he played twenty-seven holes of golf, had a peaceful dinner, and passed away. It was another divine reminder for us Shanahans that life is precious, and we must love every day.

Chapter 29

God's Gift of Marriage

IN 2004, TRACY was on a different path. She exited the academic world and pursued pharmaceutical sales. She wanted more money. At the time, we were living humbly in a new condo in Chicopee, Massachusetts.

My sobriety was trusted. It was time to return to New Orleans before she began her lengthy pharma training. We had a romantic plan that included good Cajun food, great music, and plenty of love.

We spent our nights relaxing, instead of bar hopping. The last day of the Jazz Fest was canceled due to lightning storms; therefore, we attended an amazing Jazz brunch at the famous Three Sisters Restaurant in the historic section of the French Quarter. With a full belly and a relaxed heart, we retreated back to our hotel. Sleeping together on our last night made a divine difference in our lives.

The next morning, we packed up our luggage, safely stored away some new art, but departed Louisiana with unexpected valuables. A few weeks later, we discovered that Tracy was pregnant.

The glorious news of Tracy's pregnancy prompted us to move into a safe family neighborhood. I must admit, it was an uncomfortable move for me as an Irish Catholic Holyoke native. We bought a tiny overpriced house in a predominantly Jewish city. We basically shared a driveway with our neighbor and had a small backyard with no privacy. But it was walking and bike riding distance to an elementary school that reminded me of Highland School in Holyoke. Also, it was only three miles to the Temple Beth El where the Curtis Blake Day school was. It definitely had its benefits.

Chapter 30

A Broken Curse

TO CLOSE OUT a beautiful autumn, the Red Sox came back from three games down to their archrival, the New York Yankees. They went on to defeat the St. Louis Cardinals and won their first world series since trading Babe Ruth to the Yankees in 1918. They broke the curse! It was a celebration for all fans, including the young and especially the old-time Red Sox fans.

Chapter 31

The Second Greatest Blessing

DURING THE LARGEST snowstorm in January 2005, I drove Tracy to Bay State Hospital in Springfield, Massachusetts. It was the same hospital where Casey was born seventeen years earlier. Tracy was brave; without medication, she delivered a beautiful healthy seven-pound baby girl at 6:12 p.m. on January 21. Our daughter, like me, was born with her umbilical cord wrapped around her fragile neck; therefore, the doctors had to immediately intervene. When they returned, Rowan was cleaned up, wrapped up like a little burrito, and her shiny silk black hair with highlights was all that we could see of her.

With over seventeen inches of fresh snow on the ground, on a bright, sunny winter day, 77 Colton Place, Longmeadow, Massachusetts, welcomed Rowan O'Connor Shanahan home safely.

Rowan's birth was another divine miracle to witness. She is God's blessing for all of us Shanahans and the Miklasiewicz family. We chose the name Rowan/Rohan before we knew the sex of our baby. The Rowan Tree has ancient Celtic roots that are characterized by its brilliant red berries at the end of summer. She is part of the rose family; now Rowan is gratefully part of the Shanahan family. Her middle name, O'Connor, was chosen to honor Tracy's mother, Joanne O'Connor.

Chapter 32

Paternity Leave and CAGS

AFTER ROWAN'S BIRTH, I returned to work for the next few months, but we decided that I would not return after my April school vacation until the following opening day in September. As Tracy began her new career in pharma sales, I became a stay-at-home proud Daddy. It was a blessing for me. Rowan and I bonded beautifully. I frequently visited the women that I worked with to show off my little Irish Colleen and to visit my students until I sensed that the principal and her self-selected court weren't too happy with me. It became known that they felt only mothers should be able to take advantage of paid "maternity" leave. Before I made my decision, I researched the paternity leave policy, and it included fathers.

I knew, when I returned in September, that it may be my last year at the Curtis Blake Day school, but I wasn't concerned, especially after receiving my certificate of advanced graduate degree on May 22, 2005. My favorite part of that graduation was that Rowan attended with her mom.

AIC grad is congratulated by his daughter.

Chapter 33

Baptism

I HAD A vision during one of my meditation sessions where all of the Shanahans walked to church together. At the time, I didn't comprehend the meaning of the vision, but I acted on it. The local Catholic Church, St. Mary's, was within walking distance of our new home; therefore, I called Father Riley, who was the resident priest, and asked him if he would baptize Rowan. I informed him that we belonged to Sacred Heart Church in Springfield, Massachusetts, but I shared my vision with him, hoping he would help us fulfill it. He responded joyfully; with much enthusiasm, he educated me that it was an old Irish custom to walk to church in Ireland.

Father Riley became extremely excited. We continued our conversation, getting to know each other, over the phone. I learned about his Irish heritage and his musical interests, playing Celtic music. I made a deal with him; if he would baptize Rowan on the upcoming Sunday, he could play his guitar at our reception barbecue in our small backyard. He loved the idea of free barbecue; that was truly the deal clincher.

I shared our baptismal plans with Rowan's godparents and told them that I chose St. Mary's Church, in honor of Uncle Billy's beautiful wife, Mary. They laughed and accepted with gratitude, but they also had a deal. The only way that they would walk to church was if Rowan wore her great-grandmother's baptismal gown. It was over one hundred years old, but great-aunt Carol, Libby's sister, kept it preserved like new.

Thine will be done, the weather on May 29 was absolutely beautiful. Even more beautiful was little Rowan O'Connor Shanahan, wearing Libby's precious gown; she looked like an ancient piece of Celtic crystal. I was a little nervous picking her up and seating her in the stroller, but she wasn't going to walk her little Shanahan self to church.

There were many blessings that took place in St. Mary's Church on that day. But the greatest blessing was after the ceremony; my mother and father were extremely happy. I had to ask, "You two look blessed. What was your favorite part? Rowan wearing Libby's gown, Father Riley holding her up in the air like a trophy?"

They both looked at me with childlike smiles and said, "PJ, the last time we were in this church, *we* got married." I had no idea. I never asked them where they got married. Wow, what a blessing it was to gather all of the Shanahans together to celebrate the most important sacrament for Rowan in the church where all the love began. In the Celtic world, the more circles completed, the fuller life is! We all departed St. Mary's Church with full hearts.

Chapter 34

Success

SURE ENOUGH, MY feelings were validated. When I returned to the Curtis Blake Day School, my principal had strict rules for me. She knew I hated rules. I obeyed the best that I could, but humbly speaking, the students suffered more than me. She wouldn't allow me to offer my after-school program, and she restricted my recess duties; basically, she tried to take all of the fun out of my job.

To agitate her even more, I entered her office without permission and confronted her. I reminded her that the kids and their parents loved the after-school program. It allowed the kids to socially interact with each other without being labeled as dyslexic. Then I asked her, "Who is going to play kickball and Wiffle ball with them during recess?" She told me that I was overstepping my boundaries. Then she proceeded to bring up an old case like I was on trial for another crime. She broke out an old newspaper and pulled out a folder from a locked cabinet. Then she lowered her eyeglasses and started reading. "On November 24, 2003, you went against my authority and completely ignored a school policy."

One of my students was the grandson of a local notorious mobster. His grandfather was executed on a school night, and the next morning, the grandson was about to board his bus with other students. When the parents saw him, they rudely but cautiously decided to drive their kids to school, leaving the grandson all alone. To make matters worse, the bus driver followed suit and told him he should get a private ride. His mother called me very upset; therefore, I went out of my way to pick him up and bring him to school. He wanted to attend, so I promised his mother that I would pick him up each morning until things cooled down.

The principal ended our conversation abruptly by saying, "You put my school at risk then, and you continued with all of your risky adventures. You will have to stay in your office and do what I tell you, or you can leave now!" I felt like I was back at Wilbraham Monson Academy on restriction.

Something about principals, I had a brief laugh on my walk back to my office. I knew in my heart that I was there for the students. I tactfully tried to explain to the elementary-aged dyslexic students that we couldn't have any more fun during or after school. They kept asking the principal anyways why Mr. Shanahan couldn't help them organize fun games during recess.

I learned a valuable lesson in the AA program. When my mind started wandering in all the wrong directions, I instantly started meditating. After a long session of meditation, I decided to write down my version of success. I intended to share it with parents and the students that were scheduled to graduate from our eighth grade program.

> Success sleeps within the heart; each kind and noble act you perform gently arouses success from her sleep. She will awake within your soul; your entire being will reveal this awakening to the world. Each mindful step you take throughout your day breeds a gap between fantasy and reality. Continue on your journey with strong faith in yourself; allow success to rest, but awake her every conscious breath you take. Sincerely grateful for trusting me with your kids, Patrick J Shanahan, 2005.

For my last eighth grade graduation at the CBD school, I printed "Success" on a bookmark and handed them out as gifts to all of the students. It was a bittersweet goodbye. With a confident resume, I walked out of the Jewish Temple Beth El into an unknown future, but I was excited to experience God's plan for me.

Chapter 35

The Interview

THE FIRST WEEKEND without a job, I decided to go golfing with my favorite golf partner, Uncle Billy. Before I teed off, he reached into his golf bag and handed me a little piece of paper. It looked like it came from a fortune cookie; actually, it read like one too. "Dream job awaits you, counselor needed on the pristine campus of Suffield Academy, free room and board with three delicious meals a day, master's degree needed, please call 1860."

At the time, he was unaware that I needed a new job. He told me that when he first read the want ad, he instantly thought of me.

After making a par on the first hole at Holyoke Country Club, I decided to call the number, expecting to leave a message. On the second ring, my interview began. I was asked personal questions, educational questions, and trivial ones; twenty minutes later, I met my uncle on the third hole. He asked me how the phone call went. I told him to give me a birdie on the second hole and turned my phone off for the rest of the round.

The clinical director of counseling at Suffield Academy, Connecticut, invited me for a campus tour and an interview with a panel of students. The karmic comedy of the invite was I went on a tour there as a behavioral student seeking acceptance back in 1983. In the meantime, I prayed that red flags didn't pop up on the clinical director's computer screen before I arrived. I was not accepted in 1983 because I was considered to be an "at-risk student!"

The night before my interview, I picked out my prep school outfit. I drove on to the well-manicured campus with my convertible top down in my Saab. With bright yellow Brook Brother's slacks on, a Caribbean blue shirt with a pink paisley tie and a fine pair of Brooks Brothers hushpuppy shoes, I walked into the counseling office. I was greeted by the dean of students, the clinical director, and six students.

For the next hour, I answered questions from the anxious teenagers about real-life teenage scenarios. The blessing was I already experienced each scenario; therefore, as a licensed counselor with years of troubled experiences, I answered honestly with a sense of humor and hope. The clinical director was busy raising her eyebrows and taking notes while the dean of students waited patiently to ask his questions.

His first question was "We plan to have you living here, running one of our dorms. What does your wife do for work?"

What a bizarre question, I thought, so I answered with humor. "She's a drug dealer." After the students stopped laughing, I clarified before the clinical director kicked me out of the interview. "She is a pharmaceutical sales rep for a billion-dollar company." This led to many other personal questions that I don't recall, but I was invited to go on the student-led tour of campus.

Part of the tour was the million-dollar sporting complex that included an indoor riflery range. Picturing students with guns carrying books across campus created awkward self-laughter. The students asked me what I was laughing about, so I shared about my intern position as a crisis counselor where they had metal detectors at the entrance of the school. They understood my sense of humor. It was 2006 (six years before the Sandy Hook shootings). After enjoying a gourmet lunch in their dining hall, I met the head chef, and he forewarned me with a smile not to call it a cafeteria.

I wrapped up my tour with another interview. This time, it was with a team of directors representing the heads of the departments that I would be working with: the health center, college counseling, and the dean's office. I kept it serious and professional, exhibiting my true interest in working there. The very next day, I was offered the position as a counselor for the upcoming school year.

Chapter 36

Healed Just in Time

BEFORE STARTING THE new job, I needed updated medical reports; therefore, I scheduled an appointment with Dr. Bob. He was well prepared as usual. He had all of my phlebotomy results in front of him, and with a big smile, he said, "You are healed."

"What does that actually mean?" I responded. He told me that my liver is fine, and my iron levels were back to normal. As a good Irish boy, I had to ask, "Does that mean I can enjoy a glass of pinot noir with my meals?"

"I suggest that you enjoy more of your little daughter and less wine, but yes, you should be fine," he concluded.

Chapter 37

Where to Live

THE NEWS OF my health and my job offer was exciting. The new job created strategic decision-making. To live on the campus of a private high school sounded like an opportunity to fulfill another Celtic circle; considering, I already tried back in 1983 and was kicked off after six months. This time, I was chosen to live there to help students. Thine will be done I truly felt, but I had a family, a house, and a very independent lifestyle.

I trusted God but didn't quite trust myself yet; therefore, I accepted the counseling position with the option of living at home for the first year. Orientation lasted three days. There were many rules, traditions, and a dress code to abide by, but it was not a uniform; therefore, I had to go shopping for funky sport coats, ties, and more colorful slacks. The students also had to wear sport coats and ties. It was an eclectic community of well-dressed people from all over the world.

During the first year, I met some amazing faculty that lived in dorms with their young children. They graciously invited us over for dinners to experience the dorm life, and Rowan became friends with their daughters. Living on campus became more appealing to us as a family, but the most influential factor was meeting Rocky. He was the director of the leadership program. He lived in a house on campus for many years and was the father-in-law of the headmaster. He held the truth of all aspects, involving working where you live. Rocky answered all of my concerned questions, but he also liked my successful experience of operating a Summer Adventure Program.

The Suffield Academy Leadership Program had a classroom in a renovated tobacco barn with an indoor rock-climbing facility. In a smaller barn, they had a dozen kayaks and canoes; at that time, they were building an outdoor ropes course that I could be trained on to use with my students. The blueprints to continue my summer adventure camps were drawn up in my head.

I truly knew it was God's will when the academy invited my family to move into the brand-new dorm that was dedicated to Rocky. The second floor apartment was twice the size of our small house in Longmeadow, had an extra bathroom, and our backyard was a hundred-plus acres of beauty. After a successful first year of counseling, we moved into the Rockwell Dorm over the summer and rented our house.

Chapter 38

Dorm and Campus Life

THE SHANAHANS BECAME the assistant dorm family, and the Selvitellis, who lived on the first floor, were the head family. Their three young beautiful kids and Rowan became close. At least thirty junior and senior girls lived in the main part of the dorm. They represented over eight different countries; we all became one big beautiful family.

The rent was free, but as we know in life, nothing is free. School started at 8:00 a.m., last class ended at 3:00 p.m., sports began at 3:30 p.m., dinner in the dining hall was from 5:00 to 6:30 p.m., then study hall was from 8:00 p.m. to 10:00 p.m., lights out 11:00 p.m. Except Wednesdays and Saturdays, school ended at 12:00 p.m., and sports competed on those days. I had study hall responsibilities twice a week that included helping students with their work and making sure all were accounted for before doors were locked and lights were off.

One weekend a month, I was on call for my counseling position. Sometimes, it was quiet, and some weekends were busy with teenage crises. Every faculty was expected to be involved with an after-school related extracurricular activity for at least two out of three seasons. I signed up for skiing and golfing. I figured I might as well enjoy what I was doing.

During the winter season, I was in charge of driving snowboarders and skiers to a nearby mountain called Ski Sundown in New Hartford, Connecticut, five days a week. It was a blessing skiing with my crew and cranking music on our rides. The ski team had races on Wednesdays and Saturdays; unlike many of the other sporting events, there were not many fans that could cheer on our Suffield Academy Tigers.

For the final championship race, I decided to borrow the mascot tiger suit, with the head included, and skied along the racing course cheering our Tigers on. I figured that one mascot was worth at least one hundred fans. I was definitely the only mascot that attended and probably the last.

My snowboarders became jealous and encouraged me to join them in the snowboard park. They heard that I could do backflips on my skis and wanted to take a video of me in the tiger suit. I succumbed to their peer pressure with no fear. As I launched off a five-foot jump and was at least ten feet in the air upside down, the tiger head shifted; I couldn't see, overrotated, and landed on my tailbone. The tiger head popped off and rolled all the way down to the bottom of the hill. It made an epic video but at a painful cost.

I knew I did some damage. The pain was excruciating, but I had a tailgate party that I was in charge of. I couldn't bend over enough to take the tiger suit off, so I cooked burgers and hotdogs for everyone, then selected two of my favorite trustworthy students to drive me to the nearest hospital. Thank God I took my own car that day.

Baystate Hospital, where both of my daughters were born, was the closest emergency room. I walked into the ER wearing the

Suffield Academy Tiger mascot suit without the head per wise rec-ommendation of my students. Out of curiosity, many heads were spinning around that day in the ER.

After five hours in the ER, I exited with pain medication and a new diagnosis that I've been called before, "A pain in the ass!" I had a doctor's note to rest and relax. It was a perfect segue into our March break. For this Irishman, having the month of March off was a bless-ing. I vacationed in Florida with Rowan to visit my mother. The best part was attending the Naples St. Patrick's parade then returning home for the famous Holyoke St. Patrick's weekend. I had one more week to recover before returning to work.

My spring term consisted of golfing five days a week, counsel-ing six, and attending many senior functions. Commencement was a three-day celebration, leading into the last week of finals for the underclass.

My mindful blueprints of operating a summer adventure camp became a reality. I recruited incoming freshmen, day students that lived nearby, and an upcoming senior as my student guide. We used the Leadership Barn for headquarters.

The ropes course was a perfect challenge by choice activity to start our mornings before we departed for afternoon kayaking, cliff diving, and many adventurous hikes. We ventured all around New England, including the border of New York and the Berkshires of Massachusetts. One of my favorites was the Bash Bish falls in Mt. Washington. We parked the minibus in New York and hiked through the woods until we crossed back into Massachusetts and enjoyed the largest free-falling waterfalls in both States. There were many differ-ent cliffs to jump off, ranging from forty feet to ten. The water was clean enough to bottle.

On the way home, I impulsively pulled into a blueberry picking patch; with handfuls of fresh blueberries, the kids reloaded the Suffield Academy minibus. I was driving on the Massachusetts State Pike, and a crazed driver passed by, flipping me off. It looked like he was calling the school number on the back of my bus, but I didn't understand why he was so mad until I saw his windshield covered in blueberries; I guess some of my kids preferred strawberries. Thank God my boss was on summer break and never received the complaint.

I planned the adventure camp in August but organized it so I would have one last week off to rest up before orientation started all over. There was plenty of time to share life with both of my daughters and Tracy. I was loving life.

Chapter 39

Good Health and Plenty of Gratitude

THE BENEFIT OF living on campus was developing genuine relationships with the students. As a counselor and a leadership teacher, there was plenty of opportunities to truly get to know each student. It was a blessing for me that they trusted my guidance with their lives, dreams, and goals. I honored each heart and gave thanks daily.

Physically, I was in great health; I used to swim early mornings with the swim team and used the gym often. It was an extremely active lifestyle.

One of my favorite nights of the school year was Suffield Academy's dance-a-thon. A team of students, with faculty participation, organized the "all-nighter" to raise funds for a worthy cause. Students suggested the cause and voted on the most relevant each year. Each event raised at least fifty thousand dollars.

The dance started at 10:00 p.m. and ended at 6:00 a.m. Faculty had to attend for two-hour blocks of time. My counseling and leadership philosophy was that I would not ask students to do something that I was not willing to participate in; therefore, I danced the entire night until the sun came up. At 4:00 a.m., I disappeared and returned at 4:20 a.m. through a side door, wearing a full inflatable leprechaun suit. My entrance song was "I'm Shipping up to Boston" by the Dropkick Murphys. That created enough Irish adrenaline to greet the sunrise. We all had the next day off.

Chapter 40

Summer of 2010

THE SUMMER OF 2010 began with promising joy. The Shanahans planned a one-week family reunion on a lake in New York. To lead into the reunion, my generous mother rented a big house on Cape Cod for two weeks. Tracy planned her vacation time so she could join us for the majority of days.

I packed my new VW Routan for the three-week adventure. With my kayak on top and plenty of beach gear in the back, we departed campus with much excitement. All of my siblings with their kids planned to meet us on the Cape.

The house was beautiful, and we all had our own rooms. It was walking distance to the beach. My sister and I were the camp counselors. We planned daily activities that included teaching the kids how to kayak, fish, crabbing, and simply relaxing on the beach.

The first Thursday, we decided to travel to Nauset beach for the big waves. My mother usually just dunked herself to cool off, but I encouraged her to join me to swim out beyond the waves. It was a gorgeous July 15 summer day. We planned to ride the four-foot waves back to shore.

As we were waiting for the perfect wave, I noticed that we were not the only ones out there; a few seals swam past us. Our decision was made for us as all of the lifeguards jumped up from their leisurely position, blowing their horns, they signaled for everyone to get out of the water. We jumped on the very next wave and rode it all the way safely to shore. Later that night, we saw the six-foot sharks on the news.

Our beach day was cut short, but it prompted Jerry, my mother, my sister's boyfriend, Dan, and I to play golf in the afternoon. Usually, we would take a golf cart, but for some reason, we decided to get some exercise and walk the eighteen-hole golf course. Jerry and I always had to feed our competitive nature; therefore, we played against each other for the nineteenth hole bar tab. It was a great round that ended with me handing over my wallet to the bartender. As we returned to the beach house, we kept our buzz going into the late hours of night.

On July 16, 2010, I woke up needing strong coffee and some personal time. My morning meditation routine was challenging with a full house of family. To rattle my nerves even more, my sister planned fake fun. At least that's what I call bumper boats, trampolines, and go-carts when I'm on a beach vacation. I had to remind myself that it was all about the kids.

I felt rushed, then we had to navigate traffic and wait in lines for each activity. It was survival mode for me that morning. The kids' laughter made it all worthwhile. Thank God it was a hot beautiful day; eventually, the kids wanted to go swimming at the beach.

After making lunch for everyone at the house, we ventured to the beach with coolers and kayaks. I felt more relaxed, especially knowing that I would get some solo time in my kayak. It was a turbulent windy day at sea, fitting for the morning feelings I already experienced. Dan decided to join me in his kayak. With a few cold beers, we paddled out beyond the waves. We were on a mission. We set our destination for the beachside bar that was at least a half mile against the wind. As we arrived, a few locals helped us drag our kayaks on shore. With a concerned smile, one of them strongly suggested that we stay awhile to see if the sea calmed down. That was our invite for our first margarita. As we ordered our second, I became inspired to cook a Mexican feast for everyone. Leaving our kayaks behind, we took our drinks to go and walked along the shoreline to our beach. As we arrived, the family was packing up because the wind was having its way with the sand. I pitched my Mexican feast dinner plan; well received, I was on my way to the grocery store.

It was a happy hour filled with much gratitude as I was able to shop for twelve Shanahans. It appeared that I was not the only one loving life; many friendly families were out shopping together.

As I exited the grocery store, I noticed a liquor store in the same plaza. I was feeling guilty about enjoying margaritas without Tracy, so I decided that I would buy some tequila and the mixers. When I walked in, I was greeted by an attractive girl handing out margarita samples. The hour was getting happier by the minute.

On my way back home, I experienced an overwhelming feeling of sincere gratitude. I was extremely thankful for my mother organizing and paying for the beach house, was truly blessed for the love Tracy, Rowan, and I shared, and I was excited to share my love of cooking with my extended family.

I walked in to find a hungry clan of Shanahans waiting for me. As I began to prepare our Mexi-feast, I had to remind them of the chef's deal: if I cooked, they cleaned. We had a large enough deck outside to accommodate all of us; so we sat outside and ate tacos, nachos, and burritos into the late day hours.

I could sense that my little five-year-old Rowan was exhausted, so as the family started to clean up my mess, I brought her upstairs for a shower and prepared her for a good night's sleep. My favorite part of the day was snuggling with her until she fell asleep. I was more of a tickling, story-telling Daddy than a book-reading one. I guess our laughter caught the attention of Tracy because she walked in asking to take over. I reluctantly gave up my side of the bed and recalled saying, "I'll be outside enjoying a cigar."

Chapter 41

Life-Changing Sunset

TRUTH BE TOLD, I initially planned to sit out on our deck and smoke a nice cigar into the sunset, no blame, just recalling my mindset on July 16, 2010. When I walked downstairs, the clean-up crew started razzing me about using every pan and pot in the house to make tacos. It was my excuse to exit out the side door to where my VW was parked. My keys were sitting on the front seat. That's how safe it was on the Cape in the summer. I decided to drive to the bayside of the Cape to see the sunset.

It was around 7:30 p.m.; I knew I had at least an hour left before the sunset. I was digging my new stereo, and the Grateful Dead was cranking my favorite song, "Eyes of the World." "Woke up to find out that you are the eyes of the world" was the verse that I remember singing out loud, thinking about a good early night's rest so I can wake up more peaceful. I got lost in the song and realized that I was driving in the wrong direction; therefore, I changed my game plan to revisit my old stomping grounds of Hyannis.

In my early twenties, the main drag of downtown Hyannis was great people watching. Since I haven't visited there in many years, I figured I would park, light my cigar, and take a stroll up memory lane. There wasn't any parking on main street, so I parked in a convenience store's lot. Trusting the Cape, I left my keys, my wallet, and phone under the front seat. It was a busy summer night with many families out, getting their licks in; with ice cream melting in the heat of the moment, the children were enjoying every second of their summer. It was a happy scene to witness.

My cigar was kicking in, and the sun was setting, so I decided to take the shorter route back to my VW. As I was walking along at summer's pace on a quiet sidewalk, wearing my Celtics' sweatshirt, a straw hat, and green high-top chucks, I felt the presence of someone approaching from behind me. When I turned around to see who it was, one of the young white kids grabbed me as his friend demanded that I give them my wallet. At first I thought it was a prank, so I responded, "Come on, you guys serious, who's videoing this?" I wiggled away from the kid's grip, and pure adrenaline kicked in as I witnessed Satan's eyes staring at me.

I told them that I left my wallet and my keys in my van. The other kid told me to shut the F up and give him my gold Claddagh wedding ring, but as he was talking, my high-top chucks took off running. When I looked back to see if they were chasing me, he pulled out a gun and fired one bullet. It sounded like a car backfired, but it felt like an eighteen-wheeler ran me over. I fell face-first into the hard-paved sidewalk in front of a closed laundromat on Barnstable Road. My eyeglasses shattered, but my vision was clear enough to see a pool of blood collecting in front of me.

In my blood, I saw a reflection. At first, I thought it was the shooter standing over me, but then I heard a gentle voice, "It's just you and I, take a breath, keep breathing. I love you, help is on the way." *Thank you, Jesus, I trust you.* My mind remained conscious and replayed the day as I prayed. *Thank you, Jesus, for allowing me to cook dinner for my family. Thank you, Jesus, for letting me tuck my sweet daughter into bed. Please forgive me for being restless and agitated in the morning. Please forgive me for leaving the house. Please forgive the men who shot me.*

My prayers were interrupted as I heard a car driving by. With the strength of the Lord in me, I was able to raise my left hand and tried to wave to the driver. On the twilight of July 16, lying face-first on a bloody sidewalk of Hyannis, I knew it would be hard to see me. As each car continued to pass by, I raised my heavy arm in the air, trusting that Jesus had a plan for me. I'm not sure how many cars drove by me that night; what I do know is God's angel, by the name of Adam, saved my life.

He pulled his car over and asked me through the opened passenger window if I needed help. I tried to yell yes, but a mouthful of blood came gurgling out of me. It was enough to alert Adam of the crisis that I was in. Then the real drama began.

He called 911! In the meantime, he asked me what happened. Adam was the first person I told that I was shot in the back. I tried to roll over on my side, but I couldn't move. I knew something really bad happened. We could hear sirens coming from many directions; my years of mindfulness training and Jesus's gentle directions kept me breathing mindfully.

Many sirens with different colored lights overstimulated my consciousness. I continued my mindful breathing as a paramedic cut my Celtics' sweatshirt off me to see where all the blood was coming from. He was the second person that I told that I was shot. They cautiously rolled me onto a stretcher and placed me in the back of a loud ambulance. That's when I became part of the sirens on the Cape. They asked me if I was robbed because I didn't have a wallet on me. I recall responding, "I thought the Cape was safe, so I left my wallet and keys under the front seat of my VW Routon parked in the convenience store lot." I was conscious enough to share my name and tell them where my family was.

Chapter 42

The ER, Hyannis Hospital

AS I ARRIVED in the ER, I was interrogated by detectives. Initially, I felt like I committed a crime. Questions were coming at me faster than the bullet that penetrated my back. The one question that still bothers me is "What were you doing in front of a closed laundromat?" I tried to answer as many as I could to help them find the shooters, but that one caused much distress. "I got shot in the back, and my fucking legs stopped running. That's where I fell face-first into the sidewalk," I responded in an angry tone.

I thought I was going to die of thirst, never mind the loss of blood. I begged for something to drink, but for some reason, the nurse said she couldn't give me anything; that's when I truly knew something was terribly wrong. I kept begging until she compromised with allowing me to chew on an ice chip. She told me she would be right back. There was much communicative medical jargon spoken about me while she was gone. The only information that I could discern was a helicopter ride to Boston. I lay there helplessly, strapped to a stretcher on my side, praying she would return. Then I saw her carrying a pink pitcher; it appeared that she was barely moving, but the pink pitcher was getting closer and closer. As she extended the pitcher toward me, I heard someone yell, "You can't go in there!" Then I recognized the voice of my older brother Jerry saying, "He's my brother, I need to see him!" That's when the pink pitcher full of ice chips launched into the air and landed on the floor in front of me. I watched them begin to melt away as they tried to hold my brother back. Then I was rushed back outside.

Chapter 43

My First Helicopter Ride

AS THEY WERE preparing me for an emergency flight to Boston, I remember saying to one of the pilots, "This was not part of my bucket list." He introduced himself, "My name is Steve, and I'll be safely transporting you to Boston for the best care in the State, try to keep yourself calm." The propellers were already fired up and were extremely loud, but as the doors closed behind me, the silence enveloped my entire being. I could hear each divine breath; as I inhaled mindfully, each exhale provided more gratitude and hope because I was still alive. The helicopter lifted upward, creating a bizarre feeling of euphoria. I felt like I was going to heaven.

The copilot assured me that it will be a short safe trip and to just keep breathing. I remembered my mother's story of my birth. Tears began to flow, so I tried to distract my mind by sharing my helicopter skiing trip with the copilot. The timing of my first helicopter ride was ironic. My good friend, who actually grew up on the Cape, was in Alaska visiting his sister who dated a helicopter pilot. Steve G., yes, the same name as the pilot, was in Alaska specifically to learn more about helicopter skiing and to plan our bucket list trip for the 2011 season. The copilot wanted to hear more but encouraged me to just focus on my breathing and save my energy. I took his advice to heart and paced my mindful breathing to the rhythm of the propellers. My mind kept flashing back to seeing the gun, so I started quietly chanting, "Maranatha, Maranatha…" until we landed.

The last thing I remember was the doors of the helicopter opened, and a gust of nasty hot wind intruded my lungs; it felt like I was choking. Then a team of medics rushed me away.

This was a new chapter in my life—the beginning.

"Help me, help me please!" I woke up all alone with a bizarre feeling. I was lying on my back, staring at my feet at the end of my bed, but my legs felt like they were up in the air. I had no clue how much time had passed by since I landed on the roof. Mary, my night nurse, held my hand and tried to explain.

She called them phantom feelings, then proceeded to tell me that the bullet penetrated my spinal cord. At the time, she couldn't tell me how much damage was done, but she assured me that she would take good care of me until the surgeon made his rounds in the morning. Mary told me that I was in Brigham Women's Hospital, the best spinal cord facility in Massachusetts. I asked her if she could pull my covers up because my arms were too heavy. She laughed and said, "Your arms are fine, it's the morphine." She told me to get some more rest.

I had a few tubes attached to my arm, a couple of bags of fluids hung from a machine near my bed, and a contraption was connected to my groin area. I knew I was in God's hands, so I prayed with much gratitude because I was still breathing on my own.

It was not a restful evening; I took morphine-induced naps, filled with crazy dreams of running off cliffs. Mary checked on me at least once an hour it seemed. Obviously, my memory is distorted, but what I do remember is not having any sensations in my legs. I kept trying to hold them down when they felt like they were up in the air. My mindfulness practice kept me sane. I returned to my breath often and refocused my attention on God's grace.

Chapter 44

The Surgeon's News

IT WAS JULY 18, 2010, many lost hours under critical blessed care, but I was conscious enough to comprehend the severity of my physical condition. When the surgeon finally made his way to my room, my father, mother, brother Jerry, my sister Laura, and my wife, Tracy, were present. Before the surgeon shared the news, my brother Jerry handed me a glass of water; it brought a smile to my face.

The surgeon had our full attention. "Mr. Boston, after many hours of surgery, your condition is stable. The bullet severed your spinal cord between the thoracic 3 and 10, and I had to perform a spinal fusion. It is a complete severance. Therefore, you will be paralyzed for life. The good news is you will be able to live, and you have full function of your arms and hands." There was a brief pause, and the room was filled with awkward silence until my sister became hysterical. The nurses, my wife, and Laura left the room so I could ask the surgeon some questions.

"I heard you say that I can live, thank you! Where does my paralysis begin? How will I go to the bathroom? Did you remove the bullet? How will I learn to live this way?" I had many questions, but those were the most relevant at that stage.

"It was too risky to retrieve the bullet when it penetrated your spinal cord. It just missed your heart and punctured your lungs then settled under your right clavicle. Eventually, it will move its way to the surface, and we will be able to remove it then. You are lucky to be alive. You are paralyzed from your chest down, and the nurses will show you how to go to the bathroom. Try to get some rest because your body is still in shock." The doctor assured me that he would keep a good eye on me but had to continue doing his rounds.

My father, mother, and brother Jerry looked at me with unconditional loving eyes and waited patiently for my response. I shared honestly, "Never mind lucky. I am blessed to be alive, thank you for being here."

They responded, "We will always be with you. We are Shanahans, but we are not the only ones here. The detectives are waiting to ask you more questions."

Chapter 45

Mr. Potato Head

THE DETECTIVES ENTERED my room in an authoritative manner. I knew they were there to help, but it was intimidating. One of them was a sketch artist. He kept asking me what size nose and ears the shooter had. I started laughing; it reminded me of playing Mr. Potato Head as a kid. They knew that I was heavily medicated, so they had to redirect my attention many times. I had to remind them that I didn't know the guys who shot me, and I only interacted with them briefly; therefore, I really couldn't tell what size nose the guy had.

The lead detective shared his theory that the shooter may be part of a gang, and since I survived, they could try to visit the hospital to kill me. That's the reason the doctor and nurses were calling me "Boston" to protect my identity. He told me that only family could visit and that my family will be the gatekeepers for close friends until they catch the guys. As they were leaving, the lead detective said, "I'm sorry this happened to you. We will do whatever it takes to find them, and they will pay for your suffering."

I responded, "I already forgave them, so I won't have to suffer anymore. God bless you, and thank you for your time. Please find them so they won't harm anyone else."

Chapter 46

My Roommate

AFTER ANOTHER DAY in critical care, they moved me into a double room with a young kid named Anthony. He was only twenty-one years old when I first met him but soon to turn twenty-two. Anthony was a hip-hop dancer and worked at a club in the Boston area. He fell from a third floor platform that he was dancing on and broke his back. They told him that it was unlikely that he would walk again.

We shared faith in God and kept our conservations hopeful. The morning of his twenty-second birthday, I organized a sunrise surprise. Our window faced the east side of Boston; therefore, I asked our nurse to open the shades so the sunrise would bless us with early light. Our nurse and the early morning custodian were present when Anthony first opened his eyes. We all sang "Happy Birthday" to him, and I played some Bob Marley for us as we had our breakfast. Later that day, some of his close friends were allowed to visit to help celebrate. It was a special day. His real birthday gift was the news that he will be transferred to Spaulding Rehab by the end of the week.

Chapter 47

The Angelic Harp

AFTER ANTHONY TRANSFERRED to Spaulding, I had my own room. One early morning, I woke from a dream to witness an elderly petite lady playing a harp in my doorway. I had to pinch myself, from the chest up, to see if I was actually awake. The harp was taller than she was. It was an angelic scene that lasted for eternity in my heart. There were no words exchanged, just a divine melodic long song then she disappeared.

I fell back asleep, but when I awoke, my nurse was there smiling, and she asked me if I enjoyed my visit. She also told me that I will be transferred to a rehab to learn how to live as a paralyzed man.

Chapter 48

Spaulding Rehab Intro

MY RESOURCEFUL DAD orchestrated a transfer from the Brigham Women Hospital to Spaulding Rehab. When they wheeled me into Spaulding, I had to laugh at the Dunkin Donuts sign in the lobby that read "Boston RUNS on Dunkin Donuts." My dad looked at me, wondering if I was crying or laughing. I was learning how to find the humor of life as a newly paralyzed young man; I will not be *running* on DD.

We were escorted to the spinal cord injury floor, and I was greeted by a team of therapists. A kind occupational therapist with compassionate energy introduced herself first, then an overly ambitious physical therapist shook my hand with an aggressive grip. I never thought that she would let go. An attractive floor nurse showed me my private corner room with a view. Thank God the window was wheelchair-friendly. I had an amazing view of the Bunker Hill Memorial Bridge.

My Dad helped me set up my room. On the table next to my bed within reach, I placed my speaker for my music, a couple of prayer books, and my St. Patrick rosary beads. He put the rest of my belongings away in reachable drawers. My dad was learning that his son lost some height over the summer.

Thank God there was only one bed. He wanted to camp out with me, but I assured him that I was going to be fine. His exit was emotional. The last thing he said was, "I love you, son. If you need me, please remember I only live in nearby Concord. I'll be here in five minutes." I asked him if he stole the helicopter; that created the laughter that we needed for a hopeful goodbye.

Chapter 49

Wheelchair Orientation

AT BRIGHAM WOMAN, I lived in a bed, and nurses cared for me. At Spaulding Rehab, I was taught how to be independent. First, I needed my own wheelchair. They sized me up, checked my weight, and measured how wide my shoulders were. It was an intriguing process.

I demoed TiLite wheelchairs, and to my surprise, they rolled easily. The kind wheelchair technician said, "You'll have to tell me how you like it. If you want to try a different model, no problem, I'm here for you." It was the beginning of an honest relationship. I rolled away like a kid on a new bike. It was my first feeling of excitement as a paralyzed man.

Chapter 50

Laughing Yoga

ONE OF THE alternative activities that were offered was wheel-chair yoga. I was recruited fairly easily by a cute girl in yoga pants. When she entered my room to ask me if I was interested in joining her yoga session, I was meditating to some peaceful music. After she apologized for interrupting me, she asked me what I was listening to and if I was willing to help her.

"How can I help you?" I asked her.

She humbly responded, "I am a volunteer yoga instructor, and I never taught yoga to people in wheelchairs. Maybe you can bring your music and guide us through some meditation to begin our session." That was the beginning of our therapeutic relationship.

The first session was a success. I helped her recruit a few more willing patients on my floor for her next offering. The night before our second scheduled session, I watched *The One Who Flew Over the Cuckoo's Nest*. It was one of my favorite movies. Spaulding reminded me of the hospital scenes in the movie, especially receiving medication and group therapy.

Eight wheelchair-bound patients showed up for our second session. The ages ranged from a nineteen-year-old boy to a sixty-eight-year-old woman; we all had different levels of spinal cord injuries. As I was guiding us through some breathing meditation, our eyes were closed, and the mood was very calm. One of the funniest scenes in the movie popped up in my memory, and I started cracking up laughing. Everyone opened their eyes and were staring at me, waiting for me to stop laughing. I tactfully explained what I was laughing about; a few of them knew the movie and started laughing with me. It was more therapeutic than mindful breathing. I asked our instructor if we could change the routine for the day, and we all shared some funny experiences that have happened since our injuries. It was extremely relieving as we induced many stagnant endorphins in our paralyzed bodies. We all agreed to call it "laughing yoga" and decided to incorporate it into our Thursday sessions.

Chapter 51

Communion and CaringBridge

ONE OF MY alternative nurses interviewed me and asked me if I wanted to receive religious visits. I told her that I usually go to church on Sundays, but I was open to receive as many blessings as I can. She asked me if I wanted a Eucharistic minister to visit me, and of course I said yes. "How many times a week?" she responded.

"Every day, if possible." I quickly and gratefully reacted to her surprising question. It was an opportunity to share my story with her, especially the part when Jesus visited me immediately after being shot.

Also, I was able to share with her that I write for therapy, and she introduced me to CaringBridge, a website for my personal journey of recovery. She instilled plenty of hope in my beginning stages of my recovery.

My first CaringBridge entry, "Here I am, it's July 29, 2010, and I've safely arrived at Spaulding Rehab, Boston, Massachusetts. I have a private room with a flat-screen TV and a beautiful view. I've been extremely excited to start my journey here. I have met Team Shanahan, and they are all enthusiastic and kind. I am truly blessed to be alive and privileged to have a chance to become a stronger human being, physically, mentally, and spiritually. I have a long journey ahead of me. My rehab stay will take me to at least the end of August. Much gratitude to all of you for your continued strength and prayers. It is truly a miracle that the bullet did not take my life. My wish is to share this beautiful world with you all."

My second entry was after my first lunch outside on the deck looking over the Charles River and watching the duckboats enter the river. It was my first paralyzed poem; I wrote it on a paper plate because I didn't have my computer with me.

Life's Greatest Gift
August 3, 2010

There was a bullet that tried to take a life,
Too blessed and too grateful,
This life sprung from a pool of precious blood.
A heart sung a song of love,
A song that continues to echo throughout this beautiful world.
I have forgiven the trigger and hugged the surgeon!
It is the breath of Jesus that flows through each vessel of my blessed life,
Through this breath I am continuously opening the greatest gift of life.

Chapter 52

Divine Visitors

TRACY AND MY beautiful daughter Rowan's first visit was extremely emotional but uplifting. Rowan thought my wheelchair was cool, especially when she sat on my lap, and I wheeled her around the halls.

My two favorite Boston visitors were friends of my brother Chris. God bless Dan Corey for delivering me fresh fruit a couple of times a week and "the senator" for giving me a gift that I read daily.

I remember when he entered my room, my mother was present. "Hey, PJ, glad you're alive, brother. Can I give you a spiritual gift?" he asked.

I responded, "You just did by visiting me, Senator." He proceeded to hand me a daily devotional book called *Everyday Is a Gift*. It has biblical passages, a reflection, and a daily prayer.

Another one of my special visitors was Jerry Donovan. At the time, he was a volunteer that visited patients and shared his story of paralysis. He was a productive paralyzed man that drove his own van and played golf. At first, I didn't want to hear about golf because I was still learning how to go to the bathroom by myself, but as time passed by, I became more interested in how he actually played, especially the part where he was able to stand up.

When I allowed him, he showed me videos of his paragolf machine, designed by Anthony Netto, another paralyzed man who was passionate about the greatest game ever played. It became a personal goal for me. Jerry also was the first paralyzed man to show me how he drove his van. He instilled much hope for my future, and I'm eternally grateful for him.

Chapter 53

Free Pass

AFTER A PRODUCTIVE few weeks of physical therapy and occupational therapy, I was given a free pass to wheel off campus. Initially, they allowed me to wheel to the Boston Garden and back for exercise. The GARDEN was at least five hundred yards away, and I wheeled to Bobby Orr's epic statue of when he scored the final goal against St. Louis to win the 1970 Stanley Cup. Each trip, I stopped and prayed for the Bruins to win another Stanley Cup, then wheeled back to Spaulding. The real blessing of those prayers was the Boston Bruins won the Stanley Cup that season 2010–2011. Of course, I took all of the credit and passed it along to God.

After I proved that I was trustworthy, Spaulding allowed me and guests to go out for a couple of hours at a time. There were many favorite trips, including Sunday Reggae brunch with my best friends from Holyoke, "they know who they are," and a special trip to Faneuil Hall with my best friend from University of Tampa, "Maz," and the Cianci family from Suffield Academy. We ate at the famous Black Rose and did some needed shopping.

I especially loved wheeling to the North End of Boston. A memorable trip was with my brother Chris and Dr. Cook, who traveled all the way from Cleveland, Ohio. Dr. Cook and I met on one of my bucket list adventures at the Pebble Beach resort area.

A story worthy of sharing. I was a solo golfer, and Dr. Cook welcomed me to play with him and his son. We had an amazing day and shared a beverage after. We never exchanged personal contact information; we just hugged and said goodbye. Eight years after our round, my brother Chris moved from the Boston area to Cleveland. He joined a local golf course and met Dr. Cook. As they were playing their first hole together, Dr. Cook had to ask him if he had a brother named PJ. They lived near each other and are best friends presently. Only God can orchestrate a relationship like that.

It was my first time seeing Dr. Steve Cook since our amazing golf round on the West coast. We laughed all the way to the North end, looking for a good Italian restaurant to eat. As I navigated the cobblestone sidewalks, I wheeled into an old friend of mine. He used to own my favorite Italian restaurant near my home called Carmelina's. He was standing outside of his new restaurant called Damiano's.

"Oh man, I was praying it wasn't you that I heard about," he said.

"I'm alive and starving, my old friend. Can you accommodate us?" I responded with a smile. His restaurant was on the sidewalk and had big open windows. As I wheeled in, I noticed Mr. Henry, one of the owners of the Red Sox, paying his bill. I decided to wheel over and thank him for the 2004 and 2007 World Series championships. There was a game that night, and I guess he was in a rush because he shook my hand then proceeded to climb out one of the open windows to exit the restaurant. Obviously, the owner thought that I scared his favorite customer away, but it provided an entertaining evening.

It prompted us to get tickets for the next night, and we all went to the game together. It was my first of many New England sporting events paralyzed.

On August 11, less than a month after the shooting, Spaulding offered to take me, my uncle Billy, and his son Owen sailing in the Boston Harbor. It was a special day, but I learned how compromised my body was. As we were sailing in the hot sun of August, my body overheated and started shaking uncontrollably. Thank God it was a short trip.

An inspiring visit and thought provoking was when three of my good AA friends from the Eye Opener group showed up unannounced. They brought a well-needed meeting to me. The best part was when one of my friends, a hair specialist, gave me a haircut as we watched a few duckboats enter and exit the Charles River. Before they departed, they gave me a daily recovery book signed by all of them.

My last visit to the North End was with my brother Jerry and his family. We went to the famous St. Anthony Feast of all feasts they called it. It was a carnival atmosphere with parades and many religious, festive people. I learned that day how to navigate around crowds in a wheelchair; it provided a form of adrenaline that I truly enjoyed.

Chapter 54

Escape from Spaulding

MY PRECIOUS DAUGHTER, Rowan, was starting her preschool, and I really wanted to be there for her. I thought that I would have been discharged by then, but I still had to prove that I was strong enough to live on my own; therefore, I orchestrated an escape plan for the day.

I enlisted my father to be the getaway driver and told Spaulding that I was going out for breakfast. He picked me up early, and we drove to Suffield, Connecticut, just in time to witness Rowan getting off her first bus ride to Kiddy College. She had no idea that I was going to be there. It was an emotional surprise for the both of us.

While I was in Suffield, I visited my new accessible dorm apartment. I forewarned the academy that I was coming and was greeted by many of my favorite staff members. My wife, Tracy, was busy preparing an accessible home for me while I was learning how to live as a paralyzed man at Spaulding. It gave us the opportunity to try out the width of the doorways, the new ramp, and my accessible bathroom. God bless Walter Foley, Mark Collins, and the maintenance team at Suffield Academy for making it all possible for my return to campus life.

Our ride back to Spaulding was filled with many emotions. My Dad and I laughed and cried all the way back to Boston. Before he dropped me off, he asked me if I was planning to return to AA. That question gave me plenty to think about. I decided to tell Spaulding the truth of why breakfast took so long. They said, "No problem, but you will have to do double physical therapy sessions so you can go home for good." It was a deal that I embraced.

Chapter 55

Miracles Happen at Spaulding

DURING ONE OF my physical therapy sessions of trying to pop wheelies while I was wheeling down a hallway, I had to stop to let another patient walk by. "Pull it over, you crazy Mick, a miracle is happening." I recognized the voice coming up behind me. It was Anthony, my roommate from Brigham Woman. He was able to walk using a stroller. I knew he was in Spaulding but us patients were so hyperfocused on our own recovery that we never interacted until that divine moment. I can't speak for Anthony, but I had a tear in my eye. "All glory to God, Anthony," I chanted as he walked past me.

Chapter 56

Exchanging Rosaries

ONE EARLY MORNING during my last week at Spaulding, I was reciting prayers on my St. Patrick rosary in my room when the Haitian custodian entered without knocking. Initially, he was apologetic for interrupting my prayers until I asked him if he prayed. He reached into his pocket and pulled out a set of wooden rosary beads from Medjugorje. We began to pray a decade together, and after, we prayed for his family in Haiti; they were still recovering from the January earthquake. I was able to express my gratitude for his work and shared my story. I taught him about St. Patrick that morning, and we decided to exchange rosary beads. Out of all of my interactions with many different nurses, therapists, and doctors, Fred, the custodian from Haiti, was my favorite.

Chapter 57

The Staircase Farewell

AS MENTIONED, MY physical therapist was an ambitious, goal-driven young woman. She had set goals for me to accomplish before I could be discharged from Spaulding. The last goal on her list was for me to wheel downstairs. I asked her why. "If you ever get caught in a fire and the elevator is broken, you better know how to roll your ass downstairs," she responded with a determined look on her face.

"So what are you waiting for? I just heard the fire alarm go off, and I want to get out of here and go home," I said. She showed me the narrow staircase that had six stairs to the landing area. I had to hold on to the railing with my right hand and bounce down the stairs using my left hand. The first three were successful, but then I lost my grip and wheeled down the last three out of control; I flipped over at the bottom but was laughing my ass off.

"That was wicked awesome, quickest time evah," she said in her Boston accent. It was time for me to pack up my room.

Team Shanahan had a packing party for me. They all walked me to the front door and yelled, "Now, get out of here and only come back to say hello." I was ready and knew in my heart that when the helicopter took flight to save my life, God took over my bucket list. All glory to God, I was excited to experience what was next on God's list for me. I silently prayed on my way home.

Chapter 58

Accommodation

I WAS SHOT in the back on July 16 but rolled back to work on September 10, four days before my forty-third birthday. The new school year was just beginning. I had to wear my body brace over my shirts; therefore, I was excused from wearing ties and sport coats. It was the beginning of many special accommodations. I was allowed to counsel students in my apartment when my body did not allow me to wheel to my office.

My job felt secure, but I felt guilty that I couldn't contribute as much as I wanted to. It was a challenging transition that only God could help me with. No one, except God, really knew what I was experiencing. My faith was strong. The real problem was I thought I was stronger and wasn't willing to hand my whole life over yet.

Chapter 59

Urinary Tract Infections and Spasticity

BECAUSE I WAS vulnerable to get bedsores, we decided to buy a new Tempur-Pedic bed. Tracy and I were out shopping for a new bed at a local store. As I was trying one out and the young salesman was delivering his sales pitch, my body started spazzing out of control. I felt like a fish out of the water, flopping around on top of this new four-thousand-dollar bed. The poor salesman thought that I was testing it out to see how comfortable the bed was. Tracy didn't know what was happening and neither did I; I peed all over the bed.

My body temperature rose quickly. It was a scary scene, but I didn't want to make it any worse. I told the salesman the bed didn't make me feel comfortable. I threw myself into my wheelchair and rolled out of the store. That was my first visit to an emergency room since the shooting. I was diagnosed with a urinary tract infection. They gave me some medication and sent me home. It took at least three days for my body to recover. That was the first of many UTIs.

We ended up buying a new Tempur-Pedic bed from a different store after I healed. It had an adjustable bed frame with a remote control to raise my feet when they swelled up; the head raised too. It was very helpful considering I was a T3 complete, which means I had no core strength to sit up on my own.

We should have bought the model that offered separate adjustable sides because every time I needed to sit up in the middle of the night, Tracy had to go for the ride with me. We didn't need the vibrating model because with paralysis comes spasticity. My paralyzed body frequently shook violently throughout the night. Most able people's muscles relax at night; mine tightens up then spazzes out. It was not conducive for an intimate night of sleep with my wife.

I knew my paralysis and the stress over the actual shooting created a strain on our marriage; therefore, I asked Tracy if she wanted to renew our vows. She accepted my proposal with love, and we called Father Farland to set a date. We planned our second wedding on Tracy's fortieth birthday, October 6, 2010. The blessing of this simple wedding was having Rowan as our flower girl; I felt confident that our marriage would survive our tragedy, even though the statistics were against us.

Chapter 60

Lovin' Life Festival

WHEN I WAS at Spaulding, my family and many friends formed a committee to have a two-day fundraiser. I accumulated over eighty thousand dollars of hospital bills that insurance would not cover; the helicopter ride alone was over five thousand dollars. I could have gone helicopter skiing in Alaska for four thousand dollars.

The committee planned an eighteen-hole golf tournament on October 22, 2010, at Wyckoff Golf Course in Holyoke. On October 23, they planned a music festival at the Holyoke Canoe Club along the banks of the Connecticut River, where I spent my childhood summers. Seven amazing bands of friends reunited to volunteer their musical talents. My brother Jerry was the president of the committee and asked me what we should call the two-day fundraiser. I said it sounds like a lot of great people will be loving life for those two days; hence, Lovin' Life was born.

October of 2010 was a festive month, filled with many blessings and a plentiful harvest of loving gratitude. All went extremely well, especially the Lovin' Life's first of many festivals. The harvest of that fall provided enough positive energy to lift all of the Shanahans up and carry us into the next year with renewed hope.

Chapter 61

The Only Evidence

AS I WAS teaching one of my leadership classes in the early spring, a student asked me what I was distracted about. I was wearing a golf shirt that day, and I could feel the bullet moving closer to my collar bone area. The "Brigham Woman" surgeon forewarned me that the bullet would work its way to the surface. My skin color was changing around the area; it actually looked like a big pimple.

I showed my students and told them about the bullet being left in my body. The inquisitive student in the front row, sitting closest to me, raised his notebook up in front of his face and said, "Look out, the bullet is going to shoot out of his body!" We were all cracking up laughing, but it created enough concern for me to go to Baystate Emergency Room after class.

After I explained the reason why I was there and shared my story with the friendly admittance lady, she became alarmed and notified the security. I was very nonchalant about my scenario until the security explained to me that since my case is still under active investigation, the bullet could be the leading evidence to catch the shooter. Security notified state police, and I was escorted into a private emergency room.

An attractive young resident walked into the room and introduced herself. She asked me if I wanted to be conscious during the procedure. I said, "Most definitely, I want to witness this bullet being extracted from my body. This will be the one and only, God willing." She looked around the room, nervously noticing the state trooper and the security guard, so I decided to share my story as she prepared all of the necessary instruments. I'm not sure if that calmed her young resident nerves down, but I assured her that I had faith in her work.

She numbed the area around the bullet and started carving through the muscle tissue. As mentioned, the bullet was near my clavicle, so she had to be cautious not to carve into the collar bone. The whole time, I was conscious and told her stories to keep her hands calm. We both paused and took deep breaths, as she carved through five layers of muscle tissue. It took at least an hour before she was able to extract the bullet. As she pulled it out of my wounded body, she showed it to me then dropped it into a plastic container; the state trooper had to remind her to write my information on the label. She handed the container to the state trooper to evaluate what kind of bullet it was. He said, "Yup, just as I expected, it's from a .38 caliber pistol. They are common among the street thugs."

The state trooper was about to leave with the only evidence and drive it to Hyannis, until I said, "Wait a minute, that's it?"

The young resident responded, "Yes, I got the whole bullet out of you."

I said, "No, slow it all down. Every movie I've seen, they drop the bullet on to a tin pan, and it makes a cool sound." They all looked at me like I was crazy. "Does anyone know what I'm talking about? Please go get the lead ER surgeon." I requested in a serious tone then proceeded to remind them that I do not plan to have another bullet extracted from my body. The young resident wasn't looking attractive anymore; she was agitated and told me that they are busy. I insisted!

Then the state trooper intervened on my behalf and said, "I'm in no rush to drive to the Cape, but it is the only evidence, and we want to solve this case for you." I told them all that I already forgave the shooter. That created more of a commotion in the small private emergency room, but the young resident left to find the lead surgeon.

A friendly doctor returned; he was about my age and knew exactly what I was referring to. With a smile and tweezers in his hand, he pulled the .38 out of the plastic container, held it about six inches in the air, and dropped it on to a tin pan. *Ching, ching*—it made the exact noise that I was talking about. They all looked at me, waiting for my reaction. "Now, that's what I'm talking about. Okay, State Trooper, God's speed and tell the detective I say hello and good luck."

About a month later, I was attending a concert in Northampton, Massachusetts. As I wheeled into the bar area, the young resident, looking attractive again, yelled, "Oh my god, there he is." She was retelling her version of the story to her girlfriends as I wheeled in. I bought them all a drink and reintroduced myself. We all had a few laughs and danced together during the concert.

Chapter 62

The Scene of the Crime

I HAD A few interviews after the shooting. When you Google "Patrick Shanahan Cape Cod shooting," *MassLive, Cape Cod Times*, and *Journal Inquirer* have well-written articles. But the video interview by Cape Cod Times was the most emotional and revealed all.

Rowan and I visited the scene of the crime on August 11, 2011, to honor my one-year anniversary of the shooting. It was during the day, and I was amazed at how busy Barnstable Road was. To be honest, I cannot really say that it was a revisit; the actual shooting happened so quick, and the area around where it happened was a blur. The videographer and the Cape Cod Times reporter walked with Rowan and I as I retraced the route I took to get back to my van on July 16, 2010. Rowan was an amazing and brave spirit. I do not want to be the guy who ruins a good video, so you'll have to look it up to experience the scene.

Chapter 63

Second Lovin' Life Fest and First Paralyzed Round of Golf

SINCE THE FIRST Lovin' Fest brought much joy and hope to all that participated, I decided to take it over. I changed the venue because I wanted to have bands playing while we were playing golf. My family thought that was a crazy idea considering golf is a quiet game. I laughed at that and guaranteed that everyone will love it, especially the musicians.

The Holyoke Country Club is a nine-hole golf course built near the Mt. Tom range, and it provided a natural amphitheater; therefore, the golfers could hear the music on every hole. The owner was a childhood friend; he loved the idea. I also decided that I would donate a check to a local family in crisis. I wanted to instill hope and faith in someone else's life.

The first recipient of the Lovin' Life benefit was a manager at one of our liquor stores. His house burned down on Christmas Eve, and the money provided a hotel for his family from New Year's Eve to January 2. It was enough time for the family to relax together and come up with a game plan to move into a new house. Lovin' Life became an annual event that has benefited many other families in crisis.

The best part of that second fest was Jerry Donovan; my friend from Spaulding Rehab drove his paragolfer up from Boston and let me borrow it for nine holes. I played my first paralyzed round of golf that day. It felt amazing to stand up, swing a golf club with one arm, and hit the ball 140 yards straight down the fairway. After those nine holes of playing the greatest game "evah," I announced to everyone that they will see me on the golf courses in the near future.

Chapter 64

Driving the Roads

I WAS GAINING my independence back, but I really wanted to start driving again. I needed to be able to drive Rowan places when Tracy was away; therefore, I contacted the Connecticut DMV to find out if my license was still good. They told me that I needed a surgeon's note and that I had to take ADA driving lessons. The surgeon was more than happy to write me a certified letter of approval. On the other hand, I was put on a lengthy waitlist for ADA driving lessons. Every time that I called to check what number I was, they told me that it will be a while.

A couple of months went by, and I was getting irritated so I prayed on it, "God, please guide me back to the roads of life so I can be more useful for my family. Thine Will be done." A week after I prayed, I met a retired disabled Vietnam vet that was just about to trade in his ADA Honda Odyssey van. It was equipped with hand controls and had a lift to raise me up into the driver's seat. I told him about my dilemma.

He responded, "That's bullshit, meet me at my house. I'll teach you and sell you my van for the trade-in price." I bought the van that afternoon and drove away with a huge mischievous smile on my face.

About two months later, the guy in charge of ADA driving training called me and told me to meet him in the grocery store parking lot near the academy. The day of our meeting, he expected me to be in my wheelchair. He was already there waiting for me when I pulled up in the van and told him to get in. He looked at me like I was crazy. After I explained how frustrated I was and told him my story about meeting the vet, he started laughing, then said, "I know that guy well. If he taught you, I trust you. Let's take a ride." Before we drove away, I showed him that I can use both of my hands and told him that I've been driving for a couple of months. That eased his mind a little.

I drove him around the campus, showed him how I got in and out of the van, then he signed the relevant papers for me. After getting a new ADA license, I was a legitimate paralyzed driver.

Chapter 65

God's Bucket List Cont.

NOVEMBER 26, 2011, I married my sister. Every time that I share my experience of actually being the justice of peace for my little sister Laura's wedding, I begin by saying, "I married my sister." It definitely captures the listener's attention. Laura is the author of "By the Light of My Brother's Smile," which serves as the foreword of my memoir. The brother-sister bond has always been a blessing for me.

Being a justice of the peace was never on my bucket list; therefore, I knew, when my sister asked me, that it was God intervening once again. As the true author of our lives, God was revealing a new chapter for me. I sensed a divine purpose for my paralysis. Just the title "justice of the peace" was an honor and a blessing. But to actually perform the divine sacrament of marrying two people who love each other brought divine purpose to my life. She married a hard-working, good soul; I felt confident their love shall remain eternal.

Chapter 66

Driving the Fairways

AS THE SPRING arrived in 2012, I was on a roll, no pun intended. I set my mind and aligned my will with God. I really wanted to get my own paragolfer; therefore, I prayed that God would guide me. I received a letter in the mail within a week after I prayed. It was from an ADA work agency in Connecticut. They wanted to keep me employed by helping me buy a van so I could drive to work. I called the agency to introduce myself and set a date to have a representative come visit me on campus.

In the meantime, I printed the relevant information about the paragolfer and how to purchase one. In 2012, the cost was over twenty thousand dollars, but it was cheaper than buying a new van. I was well prepared to propose my idea that they buy me a paragolf machine instead of a van.

When the very kind and compassionate representative showed up, I gave her a tour of campus. I wheeled up hills, across the main hilly campus to my leadership class, and back down Stiles Lane that had three speed bumps before arriving at my counseling office. She was tired from walking the campus and was amazed at the slope that I had to wheel around every day. I also showed her the Suffield Country Club golf course that was a half-mile away and told her that I used to be the assistant coach before the shooting. I reminded her that I lived on campus then proposed that I use the paragolfer to help me get around the campus and remain part of the golf team.

After our tour, we went over all of the legal paperwork, and she enthusiastically submitted the forms. It took two weeks to process, but they agreed to pay for my own personal paragolfer. I surprised the golf team at their first home match by showing up in my new fancy paragolfer, with golf clubs attached to the side. It was an emotional scene for all of us.

Chapter 67

Chapel Speaker and the Bird Song

IN THE SPRING of 2010, during one of my freshman leadership classes, I presented one of my poems to my class. "The Bird Song" was written when I was on paternity leave with Rowan. I wrote the poem as if the words were from Rowan.

On a warm spring night, when she was a baby, we were listening to a teddy bear song that played as I pulled its string. The teddy bear belonged to Casey, Rowan's older sister; it was at least fourteen years old but obviously still worked. After listening to the same song a few times, a bluebird landed on our window sill and started singing as the sun set. Rowan's attention shifted in awe; hence, "The Bird Song."

> Oh, please don't get me wrong for I love all of
> the teddy bear songs but as the day grows long,
> there is only one favorite song, it comes not from
> within one pull of a teddy bear's string but the
> feathers on the sill that love to sing.

My lesson plan during that leadership class was about following dreams. I told my class that I believed the poem would make a good children's book, and to publish a book was a dream of mine. However, my roadblock was I can't draw. "So, do I give up on my dream?" I asked my class.

After class, one of my talented students, Cheryl Kuo, approached me and asked if she could help me accomplish my dream by drawing the needed illustrations. She showed me some of her artwork. It was beautiful; she was extremely talented, and we began our partnership.

Cheryl had many other responsibilities, so I told her that the project had no deadline. As a good Christian girl, she became more inspired and driven to complete the project after I was shot. "The Bird Song" was finally published in 2012 by King-An Publishing in Taiwan, where Cheryl's family was from. Her mother was extremely influential with the process, and I'm eternally grateful for her.

Suffield Academy honored our accomplishment by inviting us to be the guest speakers at the monthly chapel meeting. I was able to share my story of the shooting with the entire school. At the end of my story, I invited Cheryl up on stage, and she shared about our published children's book. It was less about the actual poem and more about the teacher-student collaborative effort to accomplish a dream. We received a standing ovation that day, and Cheryl walked off the stage with plenty of confidence.

I was feeling confident rolling into the month of June, preparing for a restful summer, but us Shanahans were challenged with another emotional loss; on June 26, 2012, Aunt Mary, Rowan's godmother, Uncle Billy's beautiful wife, lost her battle to cancer. Even though Mary's funeral card read, "Grieve not...nor speak of me with tears but talk of me as I were beside you. I loved you so. It was heaven here with you," us Shanahans grieved and shared divine loving support for each other. It was an emotional summer. My heart and mind was filled with sympathy and love. Only because of God and our divine faith were us Shanahans able to move forward.

Chapter 68

Motivational Speaking

DURING THE FALL semester of 2012, a psychology professor at American International College, my alma mater, recruited me to give a motivational speech to her master level students. It was a humbling experience for me to wheel back on the campus where I received my master's in educational psychology.

I shared my story and educated the students about the recovery process. The students had many great questions. They were amazed at how resilient the human body is. I had to remind them that the strengthening of the body begins with a positive mindset. What really captured their attention was my gratitude toward God. I gave all credit to Jesus for saving me on that sidewalk in Hyannis, but I sensed from the professor's nonverbal cues that I had to keep the focus on the vocational systems that helped me along the way. Humbly speaking, it was an inspiring hour. For the encore, I showed them how I transferred into my new convertible Toyota Solara and demonstrated how the hand controls worked. They watched me drive away with hopeful smiles on their faces.

On my ride home from Springfield, my car drove me straight to the parking lot of Sacred Heart Church. I parked and broke down crying. I always knew God was my GPS, but it was the first time in my life that the initials took on a different meaning. God's personal service became the new truth of the acronym GPS that day. I was initially planning to drive back to Suffield Academy in Connecticut, but I found myself in a parking lot of a church crying with immense gratitude for God's divine presence in my paralyzed life.

My speaking tour was just beginning. A professor from Springfield College recruited me to speak to his physical rehab students. That speech went over extremely well. He enlisted me to be an adjunct professor for the following fall term. When I asked him if he planned to retire, he confided in me; cancer was in his present, and his future was uncertain. It was an emotional exchange. I promised to keep it on the down-low and also promised to teach his fall 2013 class. "God willing for both of us," I said as I exited his classroom.

Chapter 69

Hometown Hero

I WAS NOMINATED by some precious women in my life to be honored as a "hometown hero." It was humbling, especially because the ceremony took place at the Log Cabin in Holyoke, Massachusetts. There was a selected group of us, and we represented the military, the fire department, the police department, and me, a "survivor, not a victim" of another ruthless street shooting.

My entire family, along with many friends, attended that evening. It was a night filled with much gratitude, but on the way home with my wife, I sensed a different emotion from her. I asked her if there was something she wanted to talk about. It was the first time that she truly expressed her anger over my decision to leave the Cape Cod house the night of the shooting. In other words, she said that I didn't deserve to be a hometown hero. Her energy shifted quickly, and it continued to linger around our home life. Unfortunately, I couldn't help her with her feelings but suggested that she seek counseling. "You should go back to AA," she responded!

Chapter 70

God's Bucket List Cont.

TO BEGIN THE Lent season of 2013, one of the women who nominated me as the Hometown Hero asked me to speak at her church in Springfield, Massachusetts. John 15:5, "I am the vine, you are the branches. If you remain in me and I in you, you will bear much fruit; apart from me you can do nothing." This divine passage from Saint John's gospel was my meditation that they gave me to speak about. I read it a few times when they first assigned it to me, then the passage became part of my life. It kept appearing in magazines, on billboards, etc., all the way leading up to Ash Wednesday. My wife, Tracy, Nancy, and many church patrons were present on that first day of Lent.

I began my homily by reading John 15:5, then shared a short tale to capture their attention. "One day, a young priest was looking out over his tomato garden. He heard his tomatoes arguing over who was the brightest red, who was bigger, who was the tastiest of all fruits. So he walked out to his garden and encouraged them to meditate on John 15:5, then told them to look at the vine that connected them all together. He reminded them that they are all connected to the same vine and that God had created them to have individual beauty; but that they would lose their nutritional value each time they argue amongst themselves." And yes, tomatoes are fruits. I reminded my audience with a big smile on my face.

Then I proceeded to share my story and read another important line from the passage. "Every branch that does not bear fruit, God takes away and every branch that does bear fruit, he prunes!" My homily was well received. After our Mass, we all convened and shared our blessings. I told them all that being asked to speak was part of God's personal bucket list for me.

Chapter 71

Saved the Roses

IN LATE MAY of 2013, on the day of the senior prom, I was wheeling around campus, delivering roses to the senior girls. I was excited to chaperone the prom that evening. As I was wheeling down one of the sloped sidewalks, with two dozen roses on my lap, my front wheel stopped abruptly because of a little piece of mulch that was in my pathway. I catapulted out of my wheelchair and landed on my left hip. The paved sidewalk was extremely hard that day, but I couldn't feel it. That's when you know you are paralyzed.

A few students wearing backpacks witnessed my accident and ran to my rescue. "How can we help you, Shanny," they asked in a concerned tone. I was lying on the ground with roses clutched in my arms; the thorns were digging into my forearms, that part of my body I could feel. I told them for starters, "Go get my wheelchair." We all started laughing because my wheelchair was still wheeling down the sloped sidewalk. The students threw off their backpacks and chased after my wheelchair. That provided enough time to catch my breath. As they returned, they picked me up off the ground and placed me back in my chair. With a big smile, I said, "Thank God I saved the roses."

I mindfully wheeled back to my dorm and continued to hand out the rest of the roses to the senior girls that were living in Rockwell that year. After my mission was complete, I did a full-body scan, and to my surprise, there was no evident damage. The prom was a memorable evening.

Three days later, I couldn't move my neck. It felt like I slept with too many pillows under my head. I began to get a really bad headache and knew something was wrong; therefore, I drove myself to the Baystate Hospital ER. This time, I definitely was not wearing the Suffield Academy Tiger mascot suit.

They gave me an upper body x-ray and found nothing wrong. "Is there anything else that could be causing your pain?" the doctor asked me.

I said, "Oh yeah, I fell the other day and landed on my left hip."

"Well then, that's important to know. I'm not sure what that has to do with your neck, but let's take another x-ray," the doctor responded with a curious look on his face.

They wheeled me back into the x-ray room. The cute tech girl said, "Uh oh, did you miss me already?" As her team took a second look at my left hip, she yelled out from behind the curtain like the Wizard of Oz, "Found the problem, you broke your left hip in three places!"

"I guess you guys are stuck with me for a few days. What's for dinner?" I responded with a sense of humor, trying to lighten the mood.

They moved me into a surgical room and called in the specialist. I had to wait awhile, but eventually, the anesthesiologist walked in to give his pitch. After all of his warnings and prep talk, he asked, "Do you have any questions?"

"Yes, Doctor. Do I get a lollypop if I can spell *anesthesiologist* correctly? I think I got it right. I've seen too many of you guys over the past few years." We laughed together on the way to the next surgical table.

The kind orthopedist introduced himself then asked me how many screws I wanted. I told him that I golf and to put an extra in there so I can get a few more yards down the fairway. He agreed to put three screws in but forewarned me that I wouldn't be able to play for at least another year. That was the worst news of it all, so I thought. To add to the bad news, I missed my first commencement, but a few of my favorite seniors visited me in the hospital.

Chapter 72

Broken Hip, Broken Heart

BEFORE BREAKING MY hip, I knew the positive energy encompassing our marriage was shifting. We moved beyond survival mode to the reality side of a paralyzed marriage. Tracy expressed her frustration as we drove home from the Hometown Hero event, but I naively thought that our renewed vows would keep us bonded in a loving way for eternity.

I was definitely still partying whenever I could sneak it in. The combination of alcohol and pills made me even a little crazier than I already was. To my own defense, going all the way back to our Euro Trip, she had a good idea of how much trouble and pain I could cause to myself. But I always bounced back. I guess it was a selfish way of looking at my crises that I caused.

One of the nights that I was in the hospital, she visited me and tried to tactfully forewarn me that she couldn't take it anymore. She had enough of my shenanigans! Tracy's demeanor reminded me of the tired nurse at the end of her shift that first entered my ER room at Brigham Women's Hospital. It was Tracy's polite way of saying she wanted a divorce. I wanted to reach for the morphine button, but I knew that was part of the problem, and I definitely knew it would not take this kind of pain away.

It was a very lonely night in Baystate that evening. I cried and prayed until I fell naturally asleep. The next morning, I asked my nurse if there was a Eucharistic minister that could visit me. She said, "After I give you your morning medications, I will contact them for you."

I responded, "God is the only medicine that could heal my broken heart. Please make the call."

During the afternoon, a recognizable lady from Sacred Heart Church walked into my room. She had an angelic appearance even without a big harp. We prayed together, then she gracefully offered me the Body of Christ. We prayed some more, then I shared my recent news with her, including that I was married twice by Father Farland in Sacred Heart. She already knew about how I became paralyzed and expressed her love. I told her that because of her grace, I wanted to receive training to become a Eucharistic minister after I heal. She encouraged me to hand it all over to God and to follow up with Sister M. at Sacred Heart. Then she said, "I'll see you tomorrow, same time."

"I look forward to seeing you again. God bless you," I gratefully responded.

After she left, the Holy Spirit took over. I felt like I was floating over my bed, looking down at my wounded and broken body. My heart appeared to be bleeding out. When my consciousness returned, I was divinely encouraged to reread the entire passage of John 15, verse 2, "Every branch in me that does not bear fruit, he takes away, and every branch that does bear fruit, he prunes, that it may bear more fruit." This passage instilled much hope because I knew my heart belonged to Jesus. I prayed to God, "Please allow your son, Jesus the Christ, to continue pruning my heart so I may bear much worthy fruit for you, Amen."

When the nurse reentered my room, I asked her if there was any way that I could visit the maternity ward. I told her that both of my daughters were born there, and I wanted to meditate in the chapel. She promised that she would wheel me when the time allowed. The Holy Spirit redirected my emotions and refocused my mind on my beautiful daughters.

Chapter 73

A Divorced Dorm

WHEN I RETURNED back to campus, I tried to keep my marital separation quiet, but I lived with thirty females and another family. They knew Tracy was no longer living with us. As the counselor on campus, I had to try to remain positive and stay in control of my emotions. It was the first time during paralysis that I truly felt anger; it was a foreign emotion for my soul. It was easier to forgive the men who shot me than it was to forgive Tracy, but I knew that's what my Christian heart needed to do.

The only reprieve was the seniors had to pack up and depart the campus. I still had underclass students living in our dorm. Tracy used to help me with dorm duty at night because there was no elevator to visit the second floor girls. The first night that I tried to run dorm duty by myself was actually the first time in history that two girls fought on campus. It just happened to be in my dorm on the second floor. Not good!

After a couple of meetings, the school decided to move me across the street, into an apartment that they made accessible. They leased an accessible van to transport me to the main campus, but that took away my independence. I called my scenario "purgatory."

Because of my broken hip, the doctor's orders limited my hours of work; I had to rest my broken bones as much as possible, and I had physical therapy twice a week. I was able to manage my new schedule over the summer months, but I wanted to fulfill my commitment to the professor at Springfield College in the fall; therefore, from September 2013 to December, I counseled students during the morning hours at Suffield Academy and taught master level students at Springfield College twice a week from 4:00 p.m. to 6:00 p.m. The news of my adjunct professor role was not accepted well from the

CFO at SA. The tension from my bosses and Tracy's lawyer was not conducive for my required healing.

I trusted God's plan for me and knew that sacrifice and sufferings were going to be a part of it. I remained positive and kept my promises but prepared for my departure from Suffield Academy. I did not want to exit on a negative note; therefore, I spent as much quality time as I could with my senior advisees during the spring of 2014 and shared my gratitude with SA families.

Chapter 74

God's Bucket List Cont.

MY COUSIN BILLY Dillon asked me to be his Justice of the Peace at his wedding in the Aspen area of Colorado on May 17, 2014. It was another gift from God, especially needed during that time to remind me of my divine purpose.

The Dillons are from my mother's side of the family. Billy's grandfather was the brother of my grandmother Alice. They were the ones that first opened liquor stores in downtown Springfield, Massachusetts. The wedding was a family affair that filled my heart with many great memories. It was also my first time returning to Colorado since my steamboat days. This time I departed blessed.

Chapter 75

The Return to Holyoke

ROWAN AND I needed to find an accessible home to call our own. After a Sunday Mass at Sacred Heart, I rolled up in front of the altar and prayed for God's guidance. I took Rowan for a convertible tour of my old homes in Holyoke that day.

We drove up Fairfield Ave, took a left on Nonotuck, and drove by Grandma Libby's house. Then we visited 15 Robert Drive where I moved to in sixth grade. In my mind, I was thinking of finding a nice condo to keep life simple, but there weren't too many options in Holyoke. I had to remind myself that I just asked God for guidance; therefore, I turned on my GPS, God's Personal Service.

Shortly after, I drove through Wyckoff Park, one of the most expensive neighborhoods in Holyoke. I showed Rowan where my good friends grew up. God bless Peter and John McHugh. Dr. McHugh's palace was a huge white house nestled in the heart of the neighborhood. I showed Rowan one of the large homes that was in an old movie called *Reincarnation of Peter Proud*. As I was about to exit the Wyckoff Park neighborhood, I noticed a "For Sale" sign in front of a small humble home. The house was green, my favorite color, and the realtor was a friend of mine. I decided to call him and ask about the house. Surprisingly, he answered on the second ring. "I heard you were looking for condos, but you may like that house. I'll be there in ten minutes," my friend said in an excited tone.

While Rowan and I were waiting out in front of the house, one of the neighbors walked over. We knew each other fairly well; it was a great sign. The realtor pulled up while we were still catching up on life; the last thing Tami said was "The neighborhood would love to have you, PJ."

The best part of the viewing was the realtor remembering that the lady who used to live there needed a ramp to get in her front door. He found the ramp in the carport area, and I rolled into our new home.

It needed some ADA enhancements, but the price was right. My bid was accepted. Once again, God's blessings and part of his divine plan for me were unveiled. We moved in that summer. Moving back to Holyoke was like wheeling into Cheers; everyone knew my name, PJ, but I knew there was going to be challenges.

Chapter 76

After Hours and

THE HARDEST PART of the divorce was not living with Rowan every day. Our agreement was Rowan would sleep at my house every other weekend and one night during the school week. The nights that Rowan did not sleep over were like the old college days.

My house became the after-hours hangout, but most nights, I was all alone. It was not conducive to a healthy paralyzed lifestyle. That sounds like an oxymoron; whatever it was, it almost killed me. The disease of alcoholism reintroduced herself; the struggle was real but denied often.

There were many sleepless nights that first year living back in Holyoke. I was not the only one struggling with my health. My beautiful cousin Kara, Holyoke's 1994 St. Patrick's Colleen fell extremely ill at the age of forty-four. On September 2, 2015, Kara Shanahan died, and all of us Shanahans were shocked with heavy grief once again. We all attended her funeral services and emptied our hearts into God's hands at Holy Cross Church. Uncle Billy was surrounded by pure Shanahan love during those days, but God's eternal love and his divine mercy is the only way to move forward.

God bless Kara and Mary Shanahan. In the eyes of many, our faith was challenged, but knowing Kara was an organ donor and that three worthy recipients would live better lives because of her amazing grace only strengthened our faith in God.

On the other hand, the paralysis, the stress of grief, and my intake of pharmaceuticals and alcohol were wreaking havoc on my internal system. September is usually a celebratory month for me, but God had other plans for me in 2015.

Leading up to my birthday, I visited daily and witnessed my best friend Pete McHugh die slowly as his organs shut down at the age of forty-nine. On my forty-eighth birthday, I attended his wake and planned to be one of his pallbearers for his funeral.

As mentioned, God had other plans for me. On the morning of his funeral, while I was transferring out of my car into my wheelchair, an intense fever kicked in. My body began to tremble uncontrollably, and I was rushed to the ER at Holyoke Hospital. I obviously missed his funeral and spent a week confined in a sterile hospital room. I was diagnosed with C. diff. It was highly contagious; visitors had to wear toxic protective gowns to come see me. I was discharged with more drugs to take and forewarned that C. diff may become part of my struggles.

The next episode happened six months later, on the Friday of my favorite holiday weekend in Holyoke. The famous St. Patrick's weekend festivities were just beginning. My room at Holyoke Hospital was on the road race and parade route. I put signs up in my window to cheer everyone on as I remained in solitary confinement. During those lonely sick days, I had many intimate conversations with God. He told me that intense pruning was needed in my life.

Chapter 77

Return to AA

THIS TIME IT wasn't doctor's orders. I was following God's will. On January 1, 2017, I asked a couple of strong AA members to carry me down five stairs into the basement of a Holyoke Church for the "nooner" AA meeting. During that meeting, I surrendered my will to the care of God and admitted that I was powerless over alcohol. When it was my turn to speak, I gratefully said, "My name is PJ, and I'm a blessed alcoholic."

"Welcome home, PJ," one of my old customers from the Holyoke Liquor Mart responded.

Chapter 78

PJ the Leprechaun

AFTER SPENDING ST. Patrick's weekend in the hospital in 2016, I set a goal to make up for it by attending at least three parades in 2017. I planned accordingly and booked a trip to visit my mother in Bonita Springs, Florida. I knew the Florida St. Patrick's parades were scheduled before March 17, and the Holyoke parade is always after.

The first parade that I went to was on Marco Island, and I noticed many different cultures enjoying the Irish festivities; therefore, I became inquisitive and asked a married couple with their kids if they were Irish. The husband was Mexican, and his wife was from Brazil.

Their response triggered many thoughts. They told me that they loved a parade and had no idea what the divine significance of March 17 was. I continued to ask a few more people along the parade route as if I was a reporter. My findings were intriguing. Most parade attendees were Irish, but no one really knew the truth of Patrick's journey to sainthood.

The second parade was in Naples, Florida. There was definitely no one wearing Irish sweaters. We were all wearing shorts and flip-flops. It was a festive day. But again, the random attendees that I asked did not know the truth about our beloved patron saint of Ireland.

On the plane ride back home, I started writing a fictitious tale that would teach the true facts of Patrick's journey to sainthood. I created a leprechaun character and named him PJ. It was only a rough draft, but I became inspired to teach about the Christian holiday that I loved dearly.

During the Holyoke St. Patrick's parade in 2017, I fired up my paragolf machine, with an Irish flag hanging off the back of it; *PJ the Leprechaun* became a reality. I must have put at least three extra miles on my odometer that parade. The only time that I wasn't driving around blessing people was when I parked out in front of the Holyoke Hospital and recited the Chaplet of Divine Mercy for all of the patients inside.

Chapter 79

Chapel of Divine Mercy

SEEKING MERCY AND healing for my wounded body and soul during the 2017 Lent season, I wheeled along the trail of the life-size bronze Stations of the Cross at the National Shrine of Divine Mercy, Stockbridge, Massachusetts. I experienced by meditating and contemplating on the passion of Jesus, my sufferings became united with Jesus. People travel from all over the world on pilgrimage to visit the Shrine of Divine Mercy; it only took me forty minutes to drive there in my convertible.

After my first pilgrimage, I committed to make the drive at least twice a month for the 1:30 p.m. rosary and 2:00 p.m. Mass. On rainy days, I stayed inside the Divine Chapel to recite the Chaplet of Divine Mercy at 3:00 p.m.; that's the time when Jesus died on the cross. On the days that allow, I wheel along the Stations of the Cross and recite the powerful prayer of mercy that was given to Sister Saint Faustina by Jesus. There are two places in my world that I do not feel paralyzed, driving in my convertible Mustang and wheeling along the life-sized Stations of the Cross.

After I completed forty days of reciting my rosary beads for my Lent practice in 2017, Holy Mary encouraged me to continue my daily practice. By her daily blessings of grace, my paralysis has truly become a blessing for me.

Luke 5:17–26 says, "When Jesus saw their faith, he said to the paralyzed man, 'Son, your sins are forgiven.'" Saint Luke's verse inspires me to act accordingly, truly forgiven of my past sins, and to sin no more. I remain a T3 paracomplete, but I am free to enjoy heaven on earth; I am no longer paralyzed by my past.

Chapter 80

Full Circle of Life

MY NEWFOUND HEALTH and spiritual well-being created plenty of positive energy. Sobriety, one day at time, will have that effect on a willing soul. I was fueled by the Holy Spirit and no longer toxic by distilled spirits. I was praying for God's will each morning. After my ritual morning prayers one spring day, God prompted me to call the principal at Holyoke High School and ask him if he needed an extra counselor to keep the students motivated through the final month of the 2017 school year. I was willing to volunteer my time, and I let him know that my adjustment counseling license was valid.

The principal graciously invited me for a brief interview. He already knew about me, and I found out how. As we were exchanging pleasantries, one of my graduate students from Suffield Academy walked into the office; he was the principal's right-hand man. It was a divine intervention. After a short reunion, the principal handed me a walkie-talkie, told me that he'll pay me for my time, and set me free to wheel the halls of Holyoke High School.

I was able to counsel many of my Holyoke friends' kids and witness them graduate. After a successful month of counseling, I was rehired for the next school year. I am truly blessed to be able to contribute in a positive manner in my beloved community. As an eternal Purple Knight, divine purpose wakes me each morning and propels my wheels to help as many students as I can.

Chapter 81

Eucharistic Minister and a Divine Wedding

TRULY CELEBRATING MASS as a sacrifice to God and divinely participating in receiving the body and blood of our risen Lord, Jesus the Christ, in the form of the most sacred Eucharist and holy wine has transformed me. I was inspired by the grace of God and all of the Eucharistic ministers that administered communion to me while I was hospitalized to follow through with my Eucharist training. I became a Eucharistic minister just in time to be able to administer the first ever wedding in the Father Robert Wagner Celebration Center at our beloved Holyoke Jericho, "where all are welcome."

Before I share about my Uncle Billy's divine wedding, let me introduce you to Mary. The first time I met Mary was on Christmas morning in 2016 at Sacred Heart Church. After a beautiful Christmas Mass, I saw my Uncle Billy sitting in church pew 33 with an attractive lady. He already shared with me that he met Mary many months before, but it was my first blessing meeting her. I wheeled over, introduced myself, and wished them both a Merry Christmas.

As Mary and I were talking, exchanging pleasantries, something shiny from underneath church pew 33 caught the curious eye of Uncle Billy. He proceeded to climb under the pew and returned like a little joyous kid on Christmas morning. "Amazing Grace, it's a keychain with Rowan's name on it!" Godfather Billy cheerfully shared.

"Wait a minute, let me see that, that is the key to my house that Rowan lost around Thanksgiving time." I was amazed. I told them that I gave Rowan her own key to our house for a Thanksgiving gift, and she lost it shortly after.

"I guess she dropped it while sitting in church pew 33 with her grandparents, what a nice Christmas gift." Godfather Billy exclaimed. Mary witnessed a Shanahan miracle that Christmas morning.

As we exited Sacred Heart Church, Mary told me that she was excited to see her two-year-old niece Kara receive Christmas gifts. "Wait a minute, your niece's name is Kara?" I asked with a huge smile on my face. I decided to give Kara an autographed copy of my Bird Song book for a Christmas gift.

Later that week, Mary and Billy shared with more amazement that Kara's mother knew me well. Kara's mother was my assistant during my adventure camps at AIC in 2002. Only in God's kingdom can these connections happen.

On Friday, October 13, 2017, Billy and Mary got married in the humble Fr. Robert Wagner Celebration Center; it was the first wedding ever performed there. I was blessed to be one of the Eucharistic ministers. Many Shanahans received communion from me during that Mass. I'm truly happy for their marriage and wish them both many years of love and good health. The real blessing for me was feeling forgiven for sticking my fingers in the holy wine in Maine.

To close out a productive, divine-filled year, I wrote a letter to Jesus:

Dear Lord Jesus, there was a blessed time that I looked back at my footprints in the snow with awe as they filled in with fresh snowflakes shimmering with joy. Now I see only memories of legs that loved to walk. With faith I ask, do you wish for me a different path? In trust, I shall follow you knowing when I look back, my path shall be glowing with guidance for those who have lost their way; these wheels of mine are truly divine. They will guide me through each blessed day.

Chapter 82

Testimony Years

RETURNING HOME TO my birthplace, Holyoke, has been the greatest blessing God has granted me so far. His unconditional love continues to forgive my shortcomings, and his faith in me inspires my daily journey with sobriety. As each sober blessed day passes by, I think of Nickels from the Holyoke liquor mart. His willingness to allow me to guide him at that stage of my early attempted sobriety proves that where there are two or more gathered in God's name, God will bless.

It is easy for me to look back over the many years of my blessed life and see God's hands directing and redirecting my journey home. I consider Holyoke heaven on earth, and I've seen many wonderful places in this beautiful world. I contribute my feelings to coming back home to Catholicism.

With each funeral that I attend at Holy Cross Church and each wake at Farrell's Funeral home, I am always reminded of our loving consoling community and our shared divine faith; unfortunately, since I've moved back home, I am reminded way too often with many of my aged friends' deaths. There is a saying in AA, "But for the grace of God, there go I." I feel selfish saying it, so I use it to be more selfless instead. Gratitude has become my oxygen; with each blessed breath I breathe, I give all glory to God and trust that he keeps all of my deceased friends and family company.

My annual Lovin' Life golf and music fest has granted me the opportunity to help some of the grieving families through their sufferings. I realize money will never replace the loss of a loved one; my hope and prayers are that the positive energy that we generate instills faith and love in their lives.

The funerals that really penetrate my heart are from suicide; therefore, I created a daily mentality of Lovin' Life that I share by my actions and behaviors with hope that my positive resilient energy may carry a wounded soul into the next day. My business card reads, "When you are out of gas, GAS it up—*gratitude, acceptance, and self-love* will lead you to Lovin' Life.

Emptying my ego into the sacred heart of Jesus breeds humility and unconditional love in my daily life. Everything that I accomplish, every dollar earned, and each person I help is truly a blessing from God. Thine will be done, not mine.

Chapter 83

COVID Book Signing

BETWEEN WORKING AT my beloved Holyoke High School, attending weekly AA meetings, parenting a young teenager, I continued editing and seeking to write the truth of Patrick's journey to sainthood. I found a perfect publisher; Christian Faith Publishing agreed to publish *PJ the Leprechaun.*

After many months of working with CFP, all of my determination and desires came to fruition in 2020. *PJ the Leprechaun* was published before the 2020 St. Patrick's Day. It gave me enough time to organize two book signings. A dream of mine was to have a book signing at Barnes and Noble. My dream came true; the Barnes and Noble in Holyoke invited me to have a book reading and signing on the weekend before Holyoke's famous St. Patrick's festivities. Unfortunately, for all of us, COVID kicked in and canceled all parades; therefore, *PJ the Leprechaun* saved the year. The book brought much joy to many families and kept the spirit of St. Patrick alive and well. *PJ the Leprechaun* is available for sale on Amazon and Barnes and Noble. All glory to God.

Chapter 84

Tenth Anniversary Reflection

AFTER TEN YEARS, my case was closed. They never caught the two guys who shot me that night, but as mentioned, I forgave them. Now it's up to God. If I had the chance to meet them, I would let them know right away that I forgave them. Obviously, I would want to ask them why they shot me, but the truth is the answer would be for them to contemplate on. The reason is irrelevant for me. I have moved way beyond that evening only by the grace of God.

There have been many divine lessons that I've learned so far as a paralyzed man. The first one is that the only way to wheel faster in a positive direction is to let go of the past. Second lesson is to always love and forgive, even if your closest friend betrays you; the love may take on a different form, but your heart will remain pure. Third lesson is to keep a sense of humor; laughter is the panacea for all ailments. Fourth lesson is to remain positive; there is always a positive that is born from a negative situation. For example, my faith has only become stronger, and my relationship with Jesus has been more personal since the shooting. Fifth is to cherish every moment even if you end up in the hospital. That's a perfect time to express gratitude to our first responders, essential workers, especially all nurses, doctors, and custodians. This is written during COVID, and as a reminder, I'm considered to be high risk. Thank God I'm alive and able to give my own testimony. That leads me to my most important lesson, all glory to God always, remain humble servants and life will go as planned. Some friendly advice, if you are carrying any past sins, please use the act of contrition to free your soul.

Special thanks to all of my family, my friends (you know who you are), and the Lovin' Life team. Their continued support encourages me to be the best paralyzed PJ I can be. Much love always, eternal love to my beautiful daughters Casey Elizabeth and Rowan O'Connor Shanahan; they are my Coleens for life. Many blessings to my three godchildren, Matt, Lil, and Alex.

Presently, our family tree—the Shanahans: Jerry married Kim; their beautiful daughters are Kate, Abi, Lil, and Gracyn. Chris married Ali; their sons are Matt and Ben. Laura is married to Dan, and Laura's son's name is Jack. Alec married Katie, and life will unveil their blessings.

Owen Shanahan married Amy, and their blessed Ryan makes us all smile. Andy Shanahan is living his dream in Alaska. Lee Shanahan married Charlene and are blessed with Calie and Declan, Jeremy Shanahan married Mercedes and blessed with Mason and McQuaid.

On my mother's side, Brian Cavanaugh married Tatiana and are grateful for their four healthy boys, Charles, Wes, Drew, and Reese. Dan Cavanaugh married Jennifer and are blessed with Travis, Colton, and Gavin. Their sister, Meghan, married Ryan Raveis and are blessed with Eleanor, Dane, and Conor.

Josh Dillon married Daisey. Billy Dillon married Julie; she has a son named Jared.

Mary Ann McKenna married Bob Fishman and is blessed with Adam and Ian. Carol married Patrick Garrity, and they are blessed with Sarah and Nora. Sara Garrity married Kevin Sweeney and is blessed with a daughter named McKenna Marie and a son Connor Joseph. Nora is engaged to Sam Burke. John McKenna married Lisa, and they have twin boys, Michael and Nicholas.

Paul Gobeille and Charlie have a son named Joseph. Joseph married Darija and are blessed with Nikola and Malinda. Malinda married Randy Howell and are blessed with Lola, Evalyn, Valerie, Dalton and Ian. Tom Gobeille married Robin and are blessed with Samuel and Payton. Samuel is engaged to Karen. Stephen Gobeille married Corrine. Christine Gobeille married Timothy Simard and are blessed with Paige, Gabriel, Noah, and Sophie.

To all of my students, I have learned from each of you how to love, care, and provide hope for others, eternal gratitude to all of you. To my Mother Carol, your spiritual resemblance and example of Mother Mary inspire me to follow Jesus's example on a daily basis. To my Papa Jogger, your continued support and admiration to help veterans play golf and love life is inspiring. God bless you.

Chapters...

God Willing

THE LAST CHAPTERS of my life belong to the most divine author, GOD! Only by the grace of God am I able to wheel around this beautiful earth of ours.

Until we meet in person again, may God hold you in the palm of his hand. Gratefully, Patrick John Daniel Shanahan.

About the Author

PATRICK JOHN "PJ" Daniel Shanahan is a blessed father of two beautiful daughters, Casey Elizabeth and Rowan O'Connor Shanahan. He is a grateful son, brother, uncle, and godfather of three cherished souls.

Patrick has a certificate of advanced graduate studies in educational psychology. He has been blessed to counsel thousands of students from all over the world since 1999.

His personal way of overcoming adversity is through strong faith in God, loving his neighbors, and helping others overcome theirs.

Patrick's passion is writing poetry and sharing freely with those he loves and cares for. He discovered his writing voice in a creative writing course at Holyoke Community College in his beloved hometown, Holyoke, Massachusetts. He has written many poems for weddings, baptisms, birthdays, and funerals. He was the honorary poet for a neighbor's memorial golf tournament for ten consecutive years.

Patrick uses writing for his own self-therapy. After major adversity in 2010, he has published three books. *The Bird Song* was published in 2012 by King-An publishing in Taiwan. It is a short poem that helps beginner readers and parents appreciate the songs of mother nature. The talented illustrator, Cheryl Kuo, was a student of his from Taiwan. The second book *PJ the Leprechaun* was published in 2020 by Christian Faith Publishing; through the eyes of a mischievous leprechaun named PJ, true facts of Patrick's journey to sainthood are revealed.

They Called Me Boston took fifty-three years to live for Patrick and three years to write. He hopes to publish more by the grace of God.

CPSIA information can be obtained
at www.ICGtesting.com
Printed in the USA
BVHW021819130322
631364BV00027B/556